TROMPE-L'ŒIL

PAINTED ARCHITECTURE

TROMPE-L'ŒIL
PAINTED ARCHITECTURE

by

Miriam Milman

SKIRA

RIZZOLI
NEW YORK

For Boris

© 1986 by Editions d'Art Albert Skira S.A., Geneva

Reproduction rights reserved by A.D.A.G.P. and
S.P.A.D.E.M., Paris, and Cosmopress, Geneva

Published in the United States of America in 1986 by

Rizzoli International Publications, Inc.
597 Fifth Avenue/New York 10017

All rights reserved. No part of this book may be reproduced
in any manner whatsoever without permission of
Editions d'Art Albert Skira S.A.
89 Route de Chêne, 1208 Geneva, Switzerland

Printed in Switzerland

Library of Congress Cataloging-in-Publication Data

Milman, Miriam.
    Trompe-l'œil, painted architecture.

    Translation of: Trompe-l'œil, architectures peintes.
    Includes index.
    1. Architecture in art. 2. Trompe-l'œil painting.
3. Visual perception. I. Title.
ND1410.M5513 1986   758'.7   85-43549
ISBN 0-8478-0713-4

Contents

Prelude   6

1 The Suggesting of Space

Modification   9
Even before scientific perspective gave full scope to it, architectural trompe-l'œil was able to *modify* the perception of built space.

Confrontation   13
The substitution of real space by fictive space raises the problem of the *confrontation* of two conceptions of architecture.

Coexistence   15
As soon as the architectural trompe-l'œil shares the wall surface with a figural pictorial representation, their *coexistence* invites comparisons.

Designation   21
Architectural trompe-l'œil can create a symbolic space whose *function* it designates.

2 The Affirming of Space

Openings   27
By giving painters the mathematical means of rendering the third dimension, perspective enabled the painter to *open up* the real architecture and reach out to distant spaces.

Dizzy heights   32
Following the treatises on perspective which provided them with the means of doing so, artists indulged the love of *dizzy heights*.

Harmonies   37
Once distances were abolished, perspective permitted the artist to visualize the infinite. It thus made possible the creation of a crystalline and *harmonious* fictive space.

Ambiguity   44
Using the objective data of perspective, Mannerism created the semblance of a sham *ambiguous reality* that is doubly deceptive.

Exteriors   46
Short-lived decorations, the painted façades are the surface of contact with the *external world*. Their message has always been complex.

3 The Sacred Space

Amplification   51
Suggesting the past in the present, embellishing or *amplifying* a building, these were the motives behind the trompe-l'œil paintings of architecture, and the Church made ample use of them.

Transcendence   56
By breaking down the real barriers and *transcending* the limitations of matter, simulated architecture opened channels of communication between the divine and the earthly.

Humanization   63
As a mirror of reality, painted architecture in trompe-l'œil can create a setting very close at hand in which the mysteries of Holy Scripture can be pictured and *humanized*.

4 The Ludic Space

The theatre space   67
The theatrical effect was not limited to the stage space whose scenery formed the setting. To enact the fiction, the *theatre space* sometimes formed its own make-believe reality.

Seeing and being seen   71
Transformed by an architectural trompe-l'œil, the real space can in turn become a stage setting. Fictive personages placed within the painted architecture are then the attentive spectators of a play enacted for their sake. *Seeing and being seen* are part of the game.

Display and ostentation   73
From the façade, up the staircase and through the galleries to the *display and ostentation* of the state rooms, like music in mounting crescendo, the fictive spaces expand and multiply. Everything is ready for the festivities.

Evasions   82
The all-powerful illusion can break down the walls and display the fête in external spaces. Opening the windows or closing the doors, the architectural trompe-l'œil may permit *evasion* or rule it out.

Signatures   86
Remaining ambiguously anonymous, the artists sometimes sign their work with a wink of the eye.

5 Space Reconsidered

Eclecticism and dissolution   89
Eclectic and picturesque, losing the weight and volume of reality, the architectural trompe-l'œil *dissolved* in the anonymous decoration.

Another illusion   92
Dreamworlds, unfamiliar places, distant horizons, these became in the 19th century the subject of *another illusion*: the one offered to the public by museums, galleries, panoramas and dioramas.

Contestation   94
Contemporary painted walls often express the *contestation* of a certain urban architecture.

Nostalgias   96
Nostalgic, ironical, picturesque or bantering, today's trompe-l'œil chiefly answers to a desire to live in a different environment where dream and fantasy take over from the useful and uniform.

Perspectives   99
Perspective, at once constraining and liberating, is becoming again today a subject of meditation for contemporary artists.

Finale   102

Notes and References   105

List of Illustrations   111

Index of Names   115

"The simulacrum is never what conceals the truth.
It is truth that conceals the fact that there is none."
"The simulacrum is true."

Jean Baudrillard[1]

Prelude

A play of contradictions, painted architecture in trompe-l'œil utilizes the human scale in order to make its way into the world of reality. Such paintings create a fictive space which acts as a substitute for real space, building up a mysterious realm of its own, at once near and remote. In them, as he fancies, the viewer seizes on the contours of the imaginary, only to see them vanish at once into the depths of a distorting mirror. One step is enough to transform the illusion of an apparent reality into the certainty of having discovered the reality of the illusion. No question here, as in the story about Zeuxis, of testing the materiality of what has been represented. What does happen, however, is that the viewer finds himself analysing with delight the prodigies of an art whose subterfuge he fancies he recognizes even before he allows himself to be taken in by it.

Unlike the trompe-l'œil easel picture, simulated architecture does not reflect reality through a faithful and symbolic image. If it takes over the elements of reality, it does so in order to facilitate the move towards a world of illusions, which this painted architecture opens up.

The laws of perspective have given architectural trompe-l'œil the legitimacy and apparent objectivity of the rational. They let it be supposed that by piercing ceilings, by magnifying spaces and tearing

Reality of illusion

Pompeo Aldrovandini (1677-c. 1735):
Ceiling painting, Palazzo Doria-Pamphili, Rome. 1734-1735.

open walls, one can reach out to the horizon of the world and beyond, into absolute infinity. Yet, brought within the compass of the viewer, the ideal and mystical point of the infinite has never been represented; it has always proved elusive. The vanishing point, existing but invisible, accordingly remained, in Pozzo's words, "a thing of divine essence." This perpetual vanishing corresponds perhaps to a non-existence.

Architectural trompe-l'œil casts doubt on real space and its content, for it there accepts the figurative and the transcendental. It thus becomes the place of abode of living beings as well as creatures of divine essence or motionless onlookers.

So in the giddy play of alternating semblances and realities, certain acquired truths defy any challenge. On the unattainable heights of real walls, angles are conjured away, curves are effaced and details aggress the eye. Illusion or reality? Is it necessary to decide?

In the shifting kaleidoscope of these fictive constructions, reality is concealed, reason surrenders and the eye accepts the magical power of mystifying appearances.

Architectural trompe-l'œil is a fascinating game with many implications, requiring an attentive complicity to puzzle them out.

Villa of the Mysteries,
Pompeii:
Colonnades.
First century B.C.

1

The Suggesting of Space

Long before the construction of scientific perspective was able to give full scope to it, the painted architectural setting in trompe-l'œil had modified the environment by suggesting a structurally different space. A fictive space, with multiple horizon lines in which the orthogonals converged not towards a single vanishing point, but towards several vertical axes, this architectural setting was the result of a theoretically imperfect but visually puzzling illusion. Trompe-l'œil thus enriched the wall with a new dimension, opened it up, even indeed made it vanish entirely, giving the eye access to an imaginary world, beyond the limits imposed by the architecture.

In this redefinition of the wall, trompe-l'œil painting did not remain a mere decoration. By effectively establishing new relations with real architecture, it modified both its appearance and its meaning. Furthermore, the confrontation of painted architecture with the figure compositions or landscapes which they framed challenged the spectator's perception of the images represented.

Modification

Accepting the wall by emphasizing its surface—this was the simplest and oldest approach that we know of from the time of classical antiquity. At Delos, Rome and Pompeii painters thus simulated the texture and aspect of the marble and woodwork which formed the lower part of the wall. The upper part was adorned with simulated brickwork, stucco frames and friezes. In one room of the Villa of the Mysteries at Pompeii, the upper zone of the crowning is delimited by a projecting cornice on which rest brackets shaped in sweeping curves, which in turn carry festoons made up of small arches. This dynamic design imparting rhythm to the monotony of the wall remained a constant feature through the centuries, while keeping to the unbroken tradition of architectural trompe-l'œil.[1]

As soon as it was made to stand out from the wall, painted architecture fundamentally altered the structure of the spatial volume. In another room of the Villa of the Mysteries, the spectator's space is invaded by a projecting plinth—a plinth that is imaginary, like the column it supports. This device goes to create a hazy zone between the real and the sham, a fore-stage in which the spectator is caught up and turned into an actor, living out the role dictated by his everyday life in an unreal setting which is nevertheless meant to be realistic. Indeed the analogy between stage set and architectural trompe-l'œil is brought home to us at every moment. Vitruvius is the only ancient author from whom we have written evidence for the existence of a figural perspective worked out mathematically. He only refers to it in connection with scenography, which he defines as "reproduction creating illusion" and evoking in "scene painting the buildings just as they appear to us, so that what is represented on plane surfaces placed in front shall give the impression of both receding back and moving forward."[2] This balancing-out effect described by Vitruvius, between the invasion of real space and the evasion of the eye outwards, is created in the same room of the Villa of the Mysteries by opening up the top part of the wall and there depicting a temple which appears to stand back *beyond* the wall.

The closed, unlighted space of the *Cubiculum floreale* is transformed into a loggia when the wall, reduced to the dimensions of a parapet, opens on to an imaginary, enigmatic garden which does not reveal its secret.[3] A "real" garden or a pictorial "representation"? The dark ground against which the trees are silhouetted calls everything into question. A sombre vision of another world whose keeper is the serpent, this weird garden seems less real than the spur-wall which separates us from it. The latter asserts its concrete existence by a trompe-l'œil ornament representing a trellis surmounted by vases, and behind it can be seen a peaceful view of flowering shrubs. A trompe-l'œil of a trompe-l'œil, a thrusting back of the subject, this setting with its successive levels of illusion calls for an attentive scrutiny. The painted architecture of classical times, moreover, constantly elicits the complicity of the spectator. It never ceases to strike him with surprise and wonder, even though he is sometimes conditioned by being directed to the ideal position from which he can best appreciate the artful effect. Even while creating a spatial illusion, architectural trompe-l'œil appeals as much to the eyes as to the mind.

Casa del Frutteto, Pompeii:
Cubiculum floreale.
Before 79 A.D.

The ruins of antiquity have rarely left a complete ceiling decoration. Usually coated with stucco or terracotta, set out in delicate relief, such decorations took over the favourite themes of landscape and mythological figures. Nero's Golden House (Domus Aurea), the materialization of an autocrat's mad dream of grandeur, was rediscovered in the fifteenth century: it revealed the existence of a decoration simulating a ceiling with a central opening covered over by an outstretched tapestry fastened at the four corners. Evoking the *mise en scène* of the open circuses, this decoration fell in with the innovating spirit shown in the architecture of this palace where, according to Suetonius, some newfangled machinery set the constellated vault of one stately room in motion, making it revolve to the rhythm of the hours.[4] The whim of a tyrant, but also an expression of the creative powers of the best artists of the day, the decorative inventions embodied in Nero's palace certainly had an influence on Roman art, just as they influenced, over a thousand years later, the art of the men of the Renaissance who rediscovered them.

The floor of the Roman house was also decorated. The polychrome mosaic pavements usually consist of figure scenes and exotic landscapes, set out as if on a rug. Their trompe-l'œil borders, on the other hand, thanks to their density, give that sense of security which stems from the constructed element; they act as a fence or railing, preventing a lapse into the imaginary world which they frame.

Sometimes, again, the floor is covered with a monochrome mosaic, adorned in the centre with a black and white check pattern, which becomes concave or convex, empty or full, depending on the point from which they are seen: then a certain bewilderment arises, a chasm seems to open up beneath one's feet and the whole perception of space becomes elusive.

By modifying the six sides of the spatial cube, architectural trompe-l'œil as practised in ancient painting endowed the wall with a life of its own. It created a fictive world, enveloping and mysterious, suggesting both depth and movement, both interior and exterior, both dream and reality.

House of the Griffins, Palatine, Rome.
First century B.C.

Confrontation

The substitution of real space by the fictive space of trompe-l'œil raises the problem of the confrontation of two conceptions of architecture: the one expressed by the trompe-l'œil painter and the one corresponding to the material support of the painting.

As one moves from the upper zone to eye level, the forceful breakthrough of the walls in the Room of Pentheus in the House of the Vettii at Pompeii takes on an added significance and heightened intensity. It imposes upon the eye the presence of elegant buildings casting their tall silhouette against an empty sky of vivid luminosity. The contrast between this image and the simplicity of the supporting walls, pierced by a single door, makes these diaphanous buildings

seem like the "insubstantial pageant" of a dream. Yet they also evoke the House of Augustus and the Farnesina House, two of the finest buildings of contemporary Rome. This wall painting also prefigures the aspirations of urban Roman architecture in the early centuries of our era.[5] In terms of the architecture (most of it with no openings) of the provincial town of Pompeii, this painting announces the search for light through a lightening of the walls and the opening of the surfaces by the piercing of windows, thus permitting the interpenetration of interior and exterior. It also points the way to another type of town-planning, in which the houses are no longer turned in upon themselves, but open out towards the surrounding world, towards the street and town.

The advent of Christianity brought a marked change in the very essence of pictorial representation. In the framework of Christian art, spiritualized by its system of ideograms with a powerful symbolic content, painted architecture began to play a different role. It made no pretence of belonging to the real world of the spectator, but stood in the fictive world of the image represented. The spatial content of the painted architecture is progressively eliminated, even when (as in the polygonal dome mosaic of the Florentine Baptistery) it seems to stand out from the picture surface. The painted buildings usually amount to no more than abstract indications imparting rhythm to the composition and emphasizing, at the arrises, the articulations of the real walls.

In the upper transept and choir frescoes in the Upper Church of San Francesco at Assisi, the buildings painted in trompe-l'œil are brought forward from their secondary position and, as in Roman antiquity, made to play an avant-garde role.[6] Indeed, in this church, pledged to architectural sobriety by the mendicant order of the Franciscans, they introduce the florid, "modern" style of French Gothic. All along the gangway running beside the wall, the real architecture interacts with the simulated architecture. The painted Gothic gables rest on real colonnettes, and the back wall of the gallery opens on to a blue sky through a simulated arcade. For the visitor walking about the church, the holy figures seem to come to life as they appear and disappear behind the columns in a remote and mysterious middle distance. With their kinetic devices, apparently experimental in their diversity, these trompe-l'œil buildings range in boldness beyond the northern painted architecture on which they were based.

The artist who, on the wall of the Dominican church of Annecy, painted in trompe-l'œil a Savoyard nobleman's tomb, looked rather towards the past. This work was done for "Philibert, lord of Monthouz and the Isle of Annecy, counsellor of the very high and very excellent prince the Duke of Savoy, his most dread lord, and of the Duke of Burgundy."[7] According to his means and those of his church, Philibert had himself depicted with mourning figures deliberately recalling those carved by Claus Sluter for the tomb of Philip the Bold, the ancestor of his powerful suzerain.[8] The aggressively incoherent perspective of the tombstone in no way detracts from the force of the meditation proposed by the dead man's message and the tears of his companions in their lacework niches of a flamboyant but already belated Gothic. But even in its nostalgia for the past, the tomb of Philibert remains an insufficiently appreciated gem of Savoyard art, thanks to the beauty of the facial expressions and the restraint and nobleness of its grisaille.

◁ Gothic workshop:
Upper Church of San Francesco, Assisi.
View of the transept and choir.
Late 13th century.

▷ Church of St Maurice, Annecy (Haute-Savoie).
1458.

Coexistence

When the architectural trompe-l'œil shares the wall surface with a pictorial representation (figure scene or landscape), their coexistence invites comparisons. Today we tend to overlook this type of face to face, beset as we are, almost unthinkingly, by a multitude of reproductions. Because our attention is focused on the central representation, arbitrarily isolated from all that surrounds it, the simulated architecture has come to seem a subordinate setting, negligible and neglected. But this breaking up of the image does violence to the formal vision of the whole as the artist conceived it. It is an amputation on the conceptual level, for architectural trompe-l'œil is the vehicle of an objectivity conferred on it by the reality which the trompe-l'œil is designed to replace. Its confrontation

Church of San Saba, Rome.
Late 13th century.

with the "image" is therefore determinant in the perception of the degree of reality which the spectator assigns to the subject represented.

The problem was raised unequivocally in the Hellenistic period. The walls of the Room of Pentheus in the House of the Vettii at Pompeii are decorated in the central part with mythological scenes. The depiction of an imaginary world, the unreality of these paintings is emphasized by their outlines and the bright colouring of their frame. It is further emphasized by the architecture in trompe-l'œil which defines the adjacent space. Slender colonnettes jut out towards the spectator; they support an eave with a coffered ceiling. This goes to form a small building, a delicate three-dimensional shrine for the image which by contrast is identified with the plane surface of the wall. The heroes of the story are thus irrefutably banished from the world of reality.

Alongside these ensembles set in sham architecture, there arose in Roman antiquity another decoration of a diametrically opposite kind. All resemblance to reality was eliminated, and immaterial panels devoid of thickness alternate with fanciful architectural views. These latter, confined at first to the upper part of the walls, subsequently spread to the whole of them. Devoid of any rational analogy or spatial content, this pseudo-architecture was taken over and adopted by

Early Christian art. Thus, in the Catacombs, the articulations of the wall are often emphasized by decorations of a gossamer lightness.

In the face of this tendency (which may originally have expressed the taste of a sophisticated intelligentsia), the structural style persisted in Greece and Asia Minor, with, periodically, "reactionary" renascences in the Hellenistic and Roman world. The tradition of using a materialized sham architecture, serving to create a plausible space in flagrant contrast with the figure scene, seems to have been handed down through the centuries by way of the Eastern Church and transmitted to Rome in the time of Constantine.

The fragments of late thirteenth-century frescoes in the church of San Saba in Rome bear witness to this duality.[9] The representation of the legend of St Nicholas, with its figures floating among the immaterial buildings of a world in which the laws of optics and gravity are abolished, was meant above all as the intelligible illustration of a sacred text. The twisted Corinthian columns with their vigorous fluting and the arcade with its coffered ceiling, supported by brackets oriented in a central perspective, are a logical duplication of the real world: a materialization of the Church, the House of God. The coexistence of two pictorial approaches, together with our perception of the cleavage between them, go to enrich the spiritual content of each approach.

In Early Christian religious art, the frescoes superimposed along several registers were set out between a dado and a cornice in trompe-l'œil. The remains of Early Christian churches, and the later evidence of artists who copied the decoration of the early basilicas before their destruction, also show the existence of a system of colonnades between which the religious scenes were placed. It was through contact with these frescoes in Roman basilicas that the artists responsible for the nave decoration in the Upper Church of San Francesco at Assisi found their point of departure.[10] The cycle illustrating the life of St Francis is set in a series of simulated buildings remarkable for their coherent logic and flawless harmony.[11] Usually eliminated in the common run of reproductions, they are nevertheless an element of capital importance. The succession of columns adorned with Cosmati work forms a narrow passage roofed with a coffered ceiling, of a type familiar from antiquity. The perspective of the capitals and that of the brackets converge towards the middle of each stretch of wall as defined by the real engaged columns. The simulated architecture, while profoundly modifying the overall spatial conception of the church, also suggests to the spectator another way of seeing and understanding the frescoes adorning it. For as he moves about the spectator is brought to a halt by the sim-

△ Giotto (1266-1337) and his workshop:
Upper Church of San Francesco, Assisi.
Early 14th century.

▷ Altichiero (c. 1320-c. 1385):
Chapel of San Jacopo,
Basilica of Sant'Antonio, Padua.
1374-1376.

ulated architecture at definite viewpoints dictated by the perspective. It is at these stopping points that he is made aware of the content of the images, which are focused and grouped in conceptual units by the trompe-l'œil architecture.

At the foot of the gigantic, spectacular *Crucifixion* in the chapel of San Jacopo in Padua, Altichiero painted a monk kneeling in prayer before the iconic image.[12] This procedure of placing a donor — or a person making use of the image — within the picture field, while minimizing his presence, had been known for centuries. By placing the representative of the Antonites, with his imposing lifesize figure, outside the image, within a sham architecture which subtly and faithfully takes over elements of real architecture, the artist has given life to the monk, integrating him into the real world of the faithful, whose piety he stimulates by his example. The confrontation of the two images goes to establish a link between the cult object and the people contemplating it.

◁ Hall of the Barons, Castle of Issogne
(Aosta):
View of Jerusalem and Golgotha.
15th century.

▷ Giovanni del Sega (died 1527):
Hall of the Moors, Castle of Carpi
(Modena).
1506.

The artists responsible for the simulated architecture in the castles of Issogne and Carpi were apparently prompted by a similar desire to lighten the walls by opening out the interior towards the external world. At Issogne (Val d'Aosta) the trompe-l'œil executed with the meticulous care of a Flemish miniaturist represents columns of rock crystal or porphyry alternating with fine brocades: they serve to separate the real space of the spectator from the suggested landscape "outside." Behind the robust roundness of the columns, one has a view of the buildings and mountains of Savoy but also of Jerusalem and Golgotha. In the castle of Carpi, on the other hand, the room is surrounded by a narrow loggia with a coffered ceiling. Statues stand on a plinth between the pillars in the foreground. At the back, pilasters and delicate mouldings punctuate the walls over which a continuous landscape unfolds. Half hidden by the pillars, these pilasters, by their very nature, are supposed to be set against the wall.[13] They go to define it as a wall and the landscape as a picture, a *quadro riportato*. In the castle of Carpi, the wall, thrust back as it is, remains a surface indicating no spatiality; the two-dimensional landscape is identified with the wall surface.

A column in trompe-l'œil thus confers on the fresco an objective reality which a pilaster takes away. The trompe-l'œil, then, radically modifies the perception which a spectator may have of a wall painting.

Designation

Architectural trompe-l'œil, as an imaginary reality, has the power to materialize a setting which the written text can do no more than evoke. The literary reference it illustrates thus assumes the truth of actual experience, and the actor-spectator moves through a symbolic space whose function may be designated by the simulated architecture.

Painted in 1395 for the marriage of Francesco Tommaso Davizzi with Castelana degli Alberti, the frescoes in the Palazzo Davanzati in Florence transform the wedding chamber by means of a sumptuous and subtle trompe-l'œil.[14] The thick walls of the medieval palace disappear, giving place to a loggia opening on to a bucolic garden. A trellis and drapery are held by small cords to rings fastened to the edge of the wall. Lined with meniver, the precious fabric winds around the doors, allowing the flower-patterned lawn of the garden to reappear below. So the parapet wall, inlaid with marble, cannot extend down to the ground and its structure remains uncertain. Without really constructing a coherent three-dimensional space, this trompe-l'œil creates a spatial situation which acts as the setting for scenes from *La Chastelaine de Vergi*.[15]. This French poem had just been translated into Florentine. It tells the story of a gallant knight who, compromised by the advances of his lord's wife, was compelled to reveal the name of his true love, the chatelaine of Vergi. To save their honour, the two lovers put an end to their life.

Illustrating the poem verse by verse, the artist depicts the drama in terms of half-length figures, evolving with their own setting in the narrow space allowed them by the loggia. The monotonous and faulty perspective of the transverse arcades indicates, as if by a succession of arrows, the direction in which the action unfolds. Anticipating the advice of Alberti—who for "chambers where bride and groom are joined in wedlock" recommends a setting with "fine and noble" human forms favourable to the conception of lusty children—the artist illustrated for the Davizzi couple a tale with high moral implications.[16] The setting with its trompe-l'œil architecture was meant to make them share the emotions of the story and experience it as reality. As permanent spectators of a drama played out on their own walls, they saw their wedding chamber thus designated as a place consecrated to love and fidelity beyond death. As fate would have it, they themselves were caught up in a drama of real life, for five years after their marriage Tommaso Davizzi was beheaded for his involvement in a political plot. So it happens that the object and its specular reflection sometimes become one.

The thick walls of the castle of Roncolo at Bolzano appear to be hollowed out to make way for small individual rooms—sometimes communicating—which house knights and ladies elegantly dressed in the fashion of the day.[17] Posing in nonchalant and gracious attitudes, they lean on the balustrade separating them from the centre of the room. The men stand apart from the women, and on one side, in a surprising and unusual scene, some scantily clad figures are about to climb over the barrier. Tradition has preserved the name of this room: it is the *stua da bagno* or bath-

room, a designation which some art historians have thought inappropriate.[18] Yet, in the spirit of the period and under the influence of Eastern manners introduced by the Crusades, the public bath was not yet associated (as it was to be in the sixteenth century) with loose morals and vice and the spread of foul diseases. At that time courtly ablutions were of course private, or by couples, when they were haloed with an amatory or purifying symbolism. Public baths still existed in which men and women of all classes spent hours, taking refreshments to the sound of music.[19]

Castle of Roncolo
(or Runkelstein), Bolzano.
Late 14th century.

While the trompe-l'œil does not designate the castle living-room as actually being a *stua da bagno*, it certainly does allude to a place of rejoicings. By isolating it from the crowd of a public place of resort, it endows it with a fashionable elegance which it heightens by giving it the features of an ancient bathing establishment.

Indeed, in his treatise on architecture, dating back to the first century B.C., Vitruvius required of the pool that it should be "lighted from above so that it may not be darkened by the people standing about, and the walks alongside the bath must be extensive enough to accommodate those who are waiting for the first-comers to leave the bath."[20] An eagle's eyrie in the Tyrolean Alps, but also a country seat, the castle of Nikolaus Vintler, the trusted, art-loving counsellor of Duke Leopold III of Austria, may at the close of the fourteenth century have been the resort of a society of cultivated aristocrats who, by the fiction of trompe-l'œil, were able, with a wink of the eye, to partake of the joys of life of that day, purging them of equivocal allusions and lending them grace and nobility.

23

Master Wenzlaus (?):

◁ Eagle's Tower, Castle of Trento.
Month of May.
About 1400.

▷ Months of July and August, details.
About 1400.

At the top of the Eagle's Tower at Trento is a narrow room whose four sides are covered with a fresco of glowing colours. The *Cycle of the Months* represented there envelops the spectator and plunges him at once into the minutely delineated world of the late Middle Ages.[21]

The wall of the room was reduced to the size of a parapet adorned with a frieze in which portrait medallions alternate with armorial bearings. Slender twisted colonnettes rest on the spur-wall and appear at the top to support the ceiling beams. The colonnettes are the real element separating the spectator's space from the luminous, airy exterior. In this setting, governed by the cosmic laws, a continuous landscape unfolds, changing with the rhythm of the seasons. The sequence of months is marked by the alternation of the colonnettes, their name by the small plates fastened to the parapet, and the respective signs of the zodiac appear in the blue sky on either side of a bright sun. The landscape, continually changing, is animated in the foreground by the courtly and idyllic activities of the local nobility, and in the background—on successive levels up to the elevated horizon—by the labours of the peasants.

The earliest example of a cycle of the months decorating a secular space, this fresco was painted about 1400 in the international Gothic style of the period, possibly by a certain Wenzlaus, a painter recorded both in Bohemia and at the court of the Duke of Austria.[22] A fascinating set of pictures of a bygone world, this fresco also has a hidden meaning which goes to assign a precise purpose to the space it decorates.

The Eagle's Tower at Trento was built by Bishop Georg von Liechtenstein to provide accommodations for him while the castle was being restored. But when he moved back to the castle, his official residence, where he lived in pomp but under the watchful eye of his lord and enemy the Duke of Austria, he did not abandon the tower. Rather, he had it connected with the castle by a passageway built into the enclosing wall and there fitted up an antechamber for his retainers. Everything suggests that he himself sought refuge and tranquillity there, where he could enjoy himself with a small circle of intimate friends. There too, it would seem, he brought together the significant makings of a room out of which developed the iconography of the *studioli*—those cabinets given over to the studies and meditations of the intellectual. Known to have existed in ancient times, they came into fashion again in the latter half of the fifteenth century.[23] With this chamber made for the Bishop of Trento, one may be in the presence—unrecorded as such up to now—of one of their earliest and most complex examples. For the choice of a tower as a place of retreat was an allusion to the *Turris speculationis* which already in the Bible was the seat of Wisdom.[24] Standing over the town gate of Trento, it also served as an excellent post of observation. Pliny the Younger and above all Petrarch—"the king of poets" of the period[25]—describe in detail the essential conditions required by the solitary thinker for his meditations. For both these authors, aloofness was necessary but it had to be in close touch with nature, in a *locus amoenus*, a pleasant place, a haven of peace. In this isolation the sage was not alone. Pliny the Elder gave him as companions and models the pictures of his great predecessors, and Petrarch suggested a dialogue with the *gloriosi viri* of the past. For the Bishop of Trento, visual and intellectual contact with the ancients was afforded by the presence of portraits of venerable men, draped in the ancient manner, who in their small medallions adorned the parapet frieze. As for nature, it is everywhere present: it surrounds and permeates the room space with its beauties and profusion. The choice of the cycle of the months finds its explanation in the meditations of St Jerome and the writings of Petrarch. For them, the thinking mind alone can arrest passing time, in the cosmogonical alternation of day and night, of months and seasons.[26] In the end the *studiolo* in the Eagle's Tower takes on its full meaning when the complex tissue of traditions and allusions appears as a concrete reality thanks to the immaterial twisted columns and the young woman's hand which, resting against a column shaft, connects her symbolic world with that of the solitary, persecuted bishop.

Built in the centre of Florence, the palace of the Signoria could not afford the Medici any contact with nature, the essential background of the *vita solitaria* that they were supposed to lead in their *studioli*. The twelve terracotta *tondi* by Luca della Robbia, depicting the labours of the months and set into the ceiling of Piero di Cosimo's *studiolo*, had brought into this room the element of nature and also the idea of passing time. This was not the only time that a vision of nature had been introduced into the Palazzo della Signoria to embellish the study where its lords read, wrote and meditated. The mysterious *Scrittoio del Terrazzo* also has its original purpose confirmed by the hanging garden painted in trompe-l'œil on the two adjacent terraces. Of this dazzling piece of illusionism, all that now remains are the faint and moving traces of a garden bathed in an autumn glow,[27] with birds in the pergolas and the suggested murmur of fountains. Was this the *studiolo* of Cosimo de' Medici where he withdrew for undisturbed contemplation of one of his treasures, displayed in the neighbouring cabinet?[28] Or was it part of the apartment of his wife, Eleonora of Toledo, whose private chapel communicated directly with the other wing of the terrace? Perhaps this *studiolo* served as the joint study of Cosimo and Eleonora, and also as their *turris speculationis*, their secret observatory. For it has a concealed window, opening under the mouldings of the Great Hall of the Five Hundred, thus permitting the ruling couple to witness the council meetings of the people's elected representatives. Visible from the courtyard, the garden *in effigie* was doubly deceptive, since it designated as a study a space in which their overlords were free to pursue their secret purposes.

Scrittoio del Terrazzo (Terrace Study).
Palazzo della Signoria (Palazzo Vecchio), Florence.
About 1562.

2

The Affirming of Space

By giving painters the mathematical means of representing space, the theorists of the Renaissance brought about the transition from an empirical picture space, closed, fragmented and disordered, to an unlimited, unified and coherent world. From the Aristotelian cosmos built up around the centre of the earth, art passed on now to an objective, continuous, three-dimensional world where the divine presence is revealed and sublimated in the remoteness of infinity. Yet, as Panofsky has pointed out, perspective is a two-edged weapon.[1] On the one hand, it opens the picture horizon by enlarging the field of vision; it thus gives reality and weight to the objects which it places in a luminous, well-aired space. On the other hand, it imposes a constraint. By materializing the infinite at a point indissolubly linked with the human eye, it creates an unequivocal correspondence which immobilizes the spectator and conditions his visual perception.

In wall painting, the use of scientific perspective imparted its true dimension to architectural trompe-l'œil; it also carried it to its limits. By negating or amplifying the architectonic reality of the wall, when suggesting dizzy heights or creating harmonious and luminous spaces, by turns logical or incoherent, architectural trompe-l'œil utilized the new perspective space to affirm and assert the third dimension of a world designed on the scale of nature and the human being.

Openings

Medieval artists had painted church vaults blue and covered them with stars in order to suggest the contact with the celestial world. As the culmination of a complex and ambitious design, Mantegna, in the Camera degli Sposi, went counter to the architecture and pierced the ceiling of his vault. This room in the Ducal Palace at Mantua had certainly never been a wedding chamber, and the composite setting of paint-

Andrea Mantegna (1431-1506):
Camera degli Sposi, Ducal Palace, Mantua.
1461-1474.

ed architecture shows this clearly. The room space, initially blind, transformed by painting into a loggia delimited by pilasters, opens out over terraces and gardens: there unfold the episodes of the meeting of Cardinal Francesco Gonzaga with his family. The supporting wall, then, is disavowed, made away with in its entirety, in order to carry the eye into this outdoor setting. The painted pilasters support the dome of the real vault, whose structure Mantegna accepted, enhancing it with his painted architecture. The centre of the ceiling is enriched with a veritable opaion: there, around a balustrade, against a blue sky with passing clouds, the ladies of the court are portrayed, accompanied by putti poised on the heights in a precarious equilibrium.

Here, certainly, was a revolutionary innovation in the art of painting: a bold exercise of foreshortenings in accelerated perspective, but also the image of a significant space. The *mise en scène* of the reception ceremony, the presence of busts of the Caesars in the spandrels, the simulated bas-reliefs evoking the la-

bours of Hercules, the deeds of Orpheus and Arion—these constitute an exemplary evidencing and assertion of the power and glory of the Gonzagas.[2] The virtual architectural ensemble which the artist created goes to form the ideal setting for it, that of an atrium which Francesco di Giorgio Martini recommended as essential for "the houses of lords" and whose absence was, for Marc Antonio Altieri, an example of the "decadence of the contemporary nobility."[3]

This was exactly the same atrium, with its central opaion, that Mantegna had planned to build in his own house, which he had begun a few years before. Age and material difficulties prevented him from completing it.[4]

The architectural complex in trompe-l'œil which the artist painted for the Ducal Palace in Mantua was meant to glorify the political and moral power of its lord. With the actual architecture of his own home, he had intended to impress upon his contemporaries his own status as a "noble" painter, but the project proved too ambitious.

The half-obscurity prevailing in the sacristy of San Giovanni in Laterano is pierced by a dazzling light coming from the sky, and the gaze of the canons can only follow up the path opened for it in order to put it in direct touch with the divine world. By resorting to the simplest devices of perspective, in the form of glimpses of receding balustrades and putti seen *di sotto in su*, the Alberti brothers provided here one of the first and most powerful psychological weapons in the service of the Counter-Reformation ideology.[5] The negation of any connection with the surrounding architecture, and the opening of an infinite space devoid of any horizon line, make communication with the "beyond" possible. With the help of some little angels, the worshipper's soul thus finds the direction of its elevation. Yet, in the central round-window, other messengers appear in the celestial heights and penetrate the space of the sacristy. They are bearing the mitre and arms of the Aldobrandini. They thus proclaim Clement VIII (Ippolito Aldobrandini) as the absolute head of the Church, the all-powerful intermediary between man and God.

Without pretending to convey any cosmic symbolism like that of Leonardo in the Sala delle Asse in Milan, or to have the architectonic coherence of Correggio's Camera di San Paolo in Parma, the pergolas that replaced the ceilings of Late Renaissance Roman halls yet developed out of those ceilings.[6]
In the Palazzo Lancellotti ai Coronari, the heavy ceiling of one of the rooms is completely opened to the outside world. On a balustraded balcony stand some lattices which act as vine props. With extreme sparingness, they support a central round-window; above the latter, without any structural logic and from a surprising angle, a cornice on brackets is projected skywards. Elegant and luminous, Agostino Tassi's pergola transforms a closed, dark space into a bright garden pavilion. Peacock, parrot and bird of paradise emphasize the essentially secular luxury and refinement of this space. So it is that the true opening towards the "beyond" is defined by the compact circle of the round-window. The owl, its dark form seen in back-lighting against a blue sky, already belongs to this other world. Its message can only be that of Wisdom.

◁ Cherubino Alberti (1553-1618)
and
Giovanni Alberti (1558-1601):
Sacristy, Basilica of San Giovanni in Laterano, Rome.
1592.

▷ Agostino Tassi (c. 1580-1644):
Palazzo Lancellotti ai Coronari, Rome.
1617-1623.

Dizzy heights

Following the directions clearly set forth in the treatises on perspective, artists seemed to be carried away by the love of heights which they were now able to simulate. Before, the architectural barrier of the ceiling had merely been pierced. Now it exploded, and from level to level a sequence of extravagant structures was projected into the sky. The spectator, from his often exiguous standpoint, his head thrown back, his eye distraught by these staggering heights, felt at every step the threat of being crushed by the collapse of this house of cards. Despite the evidence of his eye, bewildered and mystified, he compromises with his doubts and asks no more questions about the reality of the edifice and the secular or sacred visions which loom before him in the infinite sweep of the heavens. In the thirteen vaults of Raphael's Vatican Loggie, four bays seem partially open.[7] There only remain two broad painted cross-ribs on which are depicted some *quadri riportati* illustrating the Bible. In the fields left free in the corners, we see the sky, into which is projected an architrave supported by powerful columns. With his representation of a colonnade, "on the other side" of the wall-barrier, Raphael took over a leitmotiv of ancient wall painting, as it could be seen on the upper walls of Roman houses.[8] Its integration into the ceiling enhances the space, which is thereby given a new dimension. Thus Raphael may have set out to embody the dream of a humanistic architect possessed by the idea of reviving the luxury and sweep of ancient Roman palaces, whose ruins he is known to have studied.

The issue of the dynamics of vision was also raised in the Vatican Loggie, for in order to "read" the Biblical scenes the spectator has to walk around each bay, while in order to "live" in the painted architecture he has to remain motionless in the centre of the bay.

Raphael (1483-1520) and his workshop:
Third vault, Vatican Loggie, Rome.
About 1517-1519.

Federico Zuccari (c. 1540-1609):
Room of Ganymede, Palazzo Zuccari, Rome.
Before 1603.

The Room of Ganymede in the Palazzo Zuccari in Rome is roofed with a vaulting.[9] Thanks to the devices of the painter who decorated it, the impression of curvature is done away with and the illusion seems to have been built up on a plane surface. Following up and extending the example of the Alberti brothers, Federico Zuccari pierces the ceiling like a sieve, opening up a view over a set of columns which advance and recede to the rhythm of the cornices. A second ceiling stands on this construction. Pierced with many openings, it lets the sky shine through. By the multiplication of effects and the dizzy ascension into the sky where Ganymede is being carried off by Zeus, Zuccari transformed the lower room of this palace into an ornamental tower which calls into question the dimension of its real world.

Antonio Campi (died c. 1591):
Church of San Paolo, Milan.
1588.

Raphael's example was not much followed in Rome. It was in North Italy that artists and theorists achieved the greatest "heights" of illusion. There in 1588, in the church of San Paolo in Milan, Antonio Campi adorned the barrel vault with a dazzling piece of trompe-l'œil architecture, a frankly avant-garde work.[10] Over the cornice which terminates the walls of the nave, rises a deep gallery with coffered ceiling. This gallery debouches on the church by a colonnade with Serlian motifs. The apostles present are seen *di sotto in su*; their gaze and gestures direct attention upwards. A further cornice supports a balustraded gallery with, above, a richly decorated ceiling. Powerful corbels, together with sumptuous twisted columns, give access to a third gallery, vaulted and pierced with windows. Above this, brackets and a projecting cornice seem, finally, to suggest the beginning of a ceiling. It is indeed only the suggestion of one, for this ceiling has been removed and one perceives an "external" wall alternately articulated by fluted pilaster-strips and niches housing statues of prophets.

Verbal dizziness and dizzying effects of simulated architecture... The ascension of Christ into the sky—previously a sky of intense blue—is the logical conclusion, the spiritual outcome of this endless vertical tunnel.

The loggia decorated by Giovanni Andrea Ansaldo in the Villa Negrone, near Genoa, opens out on both sides towards the garden. To emphasize this arrangement, the painter has done away with the ceiling in order to surround it with a raised loggia. Resting on brackets, this loggia penetrates the actual space. Pillars separate it from the exterior. Decorated with flowering orange trees, the loggia is animated by a picturesque world of musicians and servants, animals and birds. Above the cornice rises a parapet which, from this final barrier, affords us a glimpse of the celestial scene of Ariadne being crowned by Dionysus.

To cope with the inconvenient oblong shape of the room, Ansaldo skilfully used a perspective system with four vanishing points situated at the extremities of the central mythological picture. The spectator's eye is accordingly led to follow a trajectory which carries it from the real world of the garden loggia to the fictive realm of the airy balcony, and then, guided by the dizzy recession of the pillars, finally compels it to embrace the pictorial field of the ceiling in its totality. Reality, illusion and fiction are thus combined by the dynamics of trompe-l'œil to give vibrancy to the "erotic-naturalistic" atmosphere of this country seat of a Genoese patrician.[11]

Giovanni Andrea Ansaldo (1584-1638):
Villa Negrone, Prà, near Genoa.
1630.

Some twenty years later, Giulio Benso, the uncontested rival of Ansaldo, was called in by another Genoese family to decorate their castle at Cagnes-sur-Mer.[12] Here again we find ourselves in a space amplified in height *ad infinitum*, by means of a colonnaded loggia surmounted by a parapet which supports the edges of a ceiling widely open to the sky. Stemming from a common tradition, the formal solutions proposed by the two painters appear to be the same.[13] Yet, in some subtle ways, the options of Benso are different. By using a single, off-centre vanishing point, Benso contrives to represent only three sides of a loggia. The spectator thus receives the strongest impression of this skilful construction on entering the room. There, from the first, the surprise effect is total; it persists till the moment when, the spectator having reached the middle of the room, the asymmetry no longer makes sense. Living figures, picturesque but fixed in their immobility, are absent from this loggia which, bathed in light, has a life of its own thanks to the elegance of its vaults and the unexpectedness and vivacity of the statues adorning it. Here, moreover, the purely artistic preoccupations of a talented painter are clearly conveyed by his way of working out the tortuous, manneristic movement of the gilded satyrs that cling like creepers to the scrollwork.

As in Ansaldo's fresco, the receding columns guide the eye skywards. But in the frescoed room of the Grimaldi castle the "ceiling" is not a "picture" and its opening is not a "setting." Intent as he was on being "authentic," the painter shows the thickness of his wall and in the open sky unfolds the drama of Phaethon. The chariot is falling apart and, by a drastic foreshortening, horses and hero tumble to the earth in an implacable and irreversible downfall.

After having guided the eye upward to the heights, the trompe-l'œil delivers the message of this space. Which is, that it was Phaethon, at the head of the Ligurians, who led the Greeks to Genoa and Nice. Already in the time of the gods, then, the territory of the castle had been connected with Liguria. The overtly political symbolism also conceals an underlying moral. Too bold, too rash, Phaethon was therefore doomed. Woe to the over-bold who venture to defy authority!

Elegant and powerful, sober and luxurious at the same time, the dizzily soaring painted architecture of the castle of Cagnes is in the likeness of the noble family who commissioned it, at the height of their glory.

Giulio Benso (1601-1668):

◁ Preparatory drawing for the hall
of the Château Grimaldi.
1648.

△ Château Grimaldi,
Cagnes-sur-Mer, French Riviera.
1648.

Harmonies

Once distances were abolished, perspective permitted the eye to penetrate and visualize the infinite. The evasion it made possible took place in an objective, symmetrical and frontal space, governed by formal laws. Trompe-l'œil afforded direct access to this world, for it could enlarge the "window" opened by Alberti by imparting to it the human dimensions of actual reality. By invading the hither side of the wall, it also created a subjective and enveloping space, dense with beings and things which seemed accessible to touch. When artists felt the force of the instrument they now had in their hands, and contrived to adjust it to the features of the bearing structures, they created a new picture space, complex and harmonious, visually rich and conceptually significant.

With the Hall of Perspectives painted by Baldassarre Peruzzi about 1512, one understands the importance of trompe-l'œil architecture and its fundamental role in the definition of space. It ceased to have the secondary purpose of embellishing or thrusting back an existing wall or setting off a decorative fresco. For even if we cannot be certain of the exact role played by Peruzzi as architect in the reconstruction of the Villa Farnesina, we can nonetheless affirm that he notably enlarged the room in order to give it the proportions necessary for his perspective constructions.[14] By amplifying this representative room, the vital centre of the palace, Peruzzi allowed himself to add to it an asymmetry which derives from the position of the windows and the existing fireplace—a violation of the canons of Renaissance art which the painted architecture alone has made acceptable. Even while correcting it, the painted architecture thus subjects the real architecture to its requirements. The result makes

Baldassarre Peruzzi (1481-1536):
Hall of Perspectives, Villa Farnesina, Rome.
About 1512.

itself felt at the first glance. "The ornaments painted in perspective," writes Vasari, "appear so real that the best artists assume them to be in relief. I remember having taken Titian, one of the most celebrated painters, to see this work. He refused to believe that it was a painting; then, looking at it from a different angle of view, he marvelled at it."[15] And Serlio adds his commendation: "So artfully did Peruzzi paint the columns and other pieces of architecture that the great Aretino, so critical of painting as of poetry, declared that there was no more perfect painting in the house, despite the fact that the same house also contained some works from the hand of Raphael of Urbino."[16]

Better than Raphael, according to this stern critic. The standing of trompe-l'œil painting was thus assured. The enchantment and mystification that it gives are still as keenly felt today. Entering the room and standing at the ideal point of view chosen by the artist for his construction, one is struck with surprise. One is thus made to realize, forcefully and directly, how perfect is the spatial unity of this simulated loggia opening out on four sides over a panoramic view of Rome. With virtuoso skill, the painted pillars serve to adjust the simulated architecture to the existing walls, and these are opened up in a regular rhythm affording access, through majestic double colonnades, to a balcony running round the whole room. Alberti's precepts seem to find here their perfect illustration: "I abhor excessive luxury. I like the beauty and good taste of simple works... In the covering of walls, no pictorial figuration will be more agreeable and admired than the one representing columns of stone."[17] The transformation of the room into a loggia has not only modified the perception of space, but also radically changed the structure of the villa. Instead of being closed off around its central court, Peruzzi has opened it up towards the exterior and the city. Following a scheme of antiquity, the painter has succeeded in picturing the "ideal villa," both home and shelter, which yet allows the eye a circular flight into the distance.[18]

Here architectural trompe-l'œil assumes the dimensions of a manifesto. It is also the moment of grace when it fulfils its noblest purpose.

This privileged role played by architectural trompe-l'œil is further demonstrated in the Villa Barbaro at Maser in Venetia. Built about 1560, it was the result of a unique collaboration between three men: the client Daniele Barbaro, an enlightened humanist, the architect Andrea Palladio, an innovating theorist, and the painter Paolo Veronese, then at the peak of his mature style.[19] In his writings Barbaro combines the Aristotelian maxim of the creative experience of art with the Platonic postulate of harmony and virtue as the true underlying basis of architecture. Steeped in this doctrine and finding their sources in Vitruvius

(whom Barbaro and Palladio translated together), the client and his artists created a whole whose homogeneity and harmony stand out over and above any contradiction that may be detected in it.[20] Indeed, in the case of the villa at Maser, one is entitled to speak of a unitary iconography of architecture and painting. This villa designed by Palladio is, first and foremost, an open, airy space in which interior and exterior interpenetrate to create not only a home and residence but also a place of pleasure, rest and leisure.

''[The ancients] tried to represent the form of their buildings by the imitation of columns and their elevated projections... In the covered walks they painted landscapes representing different sites: some showing ports, promontories, shores, rivers, fountains, streams; others, temples, groves, flocks, shepherds. And in some places they painted large pictures representing the gods as they are described in fables.''[21] Veronese kept almost literally to the text of Vitruvius. He imparted rhythm to the wall surfaces by means of monumental columns, and he moved back the wall which, on a second level, opens out broadly over landscapes. Fanciful and devoid of recession, these latter become more plausible when compared with the countryside visible through the windows of the villa. Furthermore, the columns and pediments adorned with statues framing the doors go to emphasize, by their nuanced whiteness, the linear purity of these sequences of spatial breakthroughs.

Palladio's simple, well-proportioned volumes thus find their logical, visual continuation in Veronese's frescoes, while the figures peopling the setting take their place in an internal coherence which invests them with their own degree of reality.[22] The inhabitants of the villa are to be found in the gallery or in the half-opening of the doors. Their ''portraits'' can be glimpsed behind the columns, while the allegorical figures stand out from their niches or overhang the cornices. The ''icons'' bless the private spaces, while the gods of Olympus gaily people the skies over the state rooms.

Confusion and ambiguity are excluded from this limpid, harmonious world in which pure and sparing colours are combined with luminous spaces. Everywhere Veronese's painted architecture re-echoes the classical sobriety of the Palladian architecture. ''We ordinarily describe as convenient a house which is designed in accordance with the quality of its masters, and all of whose parts have not only a relation and correspondence with the whole, but also a symmetry amongst themselves,'' wrote Palladio.[23] In the Villa Barbaro at Maser the architectural trompe-l'œil ceases to be a device, a corrective or a manifesto, for it fits perfectly into the architect's vision while interpreting it. It thus becomes a coherent and constituent element of the architectural space in its entirety and acquires a new dimension. The Villa Barbaro nevertheless remains a special case.

tileschi, who are playing various musical instruments. Contemplated by servants and inspired by the Muses who figure below, in the spandrels, the music-makers appear to be producing sounds as spellbinding as the vibrant atmosphere of this room. The pinkish grey of the architecture, the pastel colours of the women, and perhaps the added mark of time and oblivion, further heighten the impression of ephemeral elegance.

As the trompe-l'œil of an improbable reality, the specular image of a bygone age, these constructions raised on a concave surface which amplifies and contracts them, deforms them and materializes them, go to create a counterpointed harmony of unmatched refinement and ambiguity.[25]

In the great hall of the Palazzo Lancellotti ai Coronari, the decoration painted by Tassi is felt from the first glance as both a visual and psychological shock and wonder.[26] Itself a source of light, the fresco lifts into the infinite the already imposing height of the wall. Severe and grandiose, the painted architecture is developed according to two orders of cross-vaulted loggias supported by pillars. Engaged columns, with twisted shafts in the upper part, Doric in the lower, punctuate the walls and perfectly integrate the painted architecture with the real structure. Beyond the loggias, one sees a continuous landscape: unfolding from one bay to the next, following the rhythm of daylight from sunrise to sunset, it represents pastoral views with distant mountains, shores and sea dotted with sailing-boats.[27] Nature here is untroubled by any human presence; but over each door a "picture" disclosed by a sham red curtain tells a story.[28] In the heights, the loges with their balustrades shelter exotic birds—the token, as usual, of luxury and refinement. This airy, luminous space, which is at once interior and exterior, evokes to the full, as never before, the intoxicating enchantment of a dream world.

Harmony and music reign in the Casino delle Muse decorated by Tassi and Gentileschi. This pavilion adjoining the former palace of Scipione Borghese was obviously devoted to the pleasures of shows and entertainments.[24] Tassi embellished the longitudinal barrel vault of the room with a painted loggia.

Supported by brackets, it opens towards the sky by means of vaults resting on pilasters. The geometry of the space, together with the necessity of allowing the fresco to be seen from the garden through the large bays giving access to it, compelled Tassi to adopt the solution of an off-centre vanishing point for his decoration. So it is that only three sides of the painted loggia are actually pictured; the one behind the spectator, over the glassed-in bay, is reduced to a simple cornice. The loges, opening towards the exterior, are peopled with exquisite creatures, painted by Gen-

The School of Bologna, famous above all others for its *quadraturisti*, had already produced such masters as Tibaldi and Gerolamo Curti. To the backbone of the Roman trompe-l'œil architectures, they added the ornaments, flowers and gildings which contributed to give them a festive air, which has since become the hallmark of their style.[29]

According to their biographer and contemporary, Malvasia, two artists of the second generation, Angelo Michele Colonna and Agostino Mitelli, were the ones who introduced "something new, the surest way of touching the human mind in its ingenuousness, which painters have always tried to arouse... Buonarroti with his 'terribilità'... Tintoretto with 'movement'... The two faithful companions Colonna and Mitelli are the leading Bolognese masters of fresco, with their lavish and lively ornaments. For in their

hands *quadratura* appeared noble and majestic."[30] Faithful companions they were indeed; an exemplary pair of collaborators such as the work of decoration seemed to require if it was to achieve its happiest effects. Colonna painted the figures and Mitelli the buildings, though sometimes their roles were reversed.

Famous in their day, they were summoned to all parts of Italy; they were even invited to Paris and Madrid. Their imprint was felt in Europe for over a century. "They left then for Florence," writes Malvasia, where they decorated rooms "whose beauty I need not point out, for we hear it spoken of every day and every hour and re-echoed, the glorious repetition of all those who pass through this majestic city and do naught but praise them, equally with the other wonders to be found there."

◁ ▷ Angelo Michele Colonna (1600-1687)
and
Agostino Mitelli (1609-1660):
Audience Chamber, Palazzo Pitti, Florence.
1636-1641.

These frescoes in Florence, already so famous at the time of their execution, decorated the audience chambers of the Grand Duke Ferdinando II de' Medici.[31] Almost overwhelming in its splendour, the painted architecture here is no longer oriented towards the exterior. It is only in the uppermost loggias, in the hollow of the vault, and in the centre of the ceiling, that some patches of blue sky appear. The simulated walls come one after another, one on top of another, without respecting the actual structure of the support. They create a space closed off by side-wings which catch the eye and lead it astray.

Coming like the manifesto for a new architecture, the monumental curving staircase anticipates a reality which only made its appearance a generation later. The distant, rose-tinted space acting as a background has the strict circular design of a pantheon, as re-presented later in Neoclassical art. The profusion of architectural forms in the foreground seems to defy probability. The eye is accordingly bewildered by monumental columns, balconied loggias, open domes, tortuous passageways; and yet they never depart from a strictly symmetrical construction which respects the rules of perspective laid down by Vignola. Muscular atlases and putti become the organic, writhing support of the upper structures. And somewhere in the heights, playlets are being acted by discreet and colourful figures.

Majestic and smiling, tranquil and impossible, monumental and dynamic, the painted architecture of Colonna and Mitelli seems to be the quintessence of a new harmony, made up of the characteristic contradictions of a style in itself controversial which may fittingly be called Baroque.

Ambiguity

A complex masterpiece, often discussed and analysed, the ceiling of the Sistine Chapel was not designed to give the illusion of a unitary reality. The fact is that the human beings represented there by Michelangelo all belong to different worlds: the heroes of Genesis evolving in their own fictive space, the marble putti, the monumental, living prophets and sibyls, and the ambiguous *ignudi*, all stand on varied levels of reality.[32] These figures are fitted into a painted architecture which, however logical in appearance, does not have any homogeneous consis-

tency. Articulated differently on two distinct axes, it is constructed with a multiplicity of viewpoints which call for a stage-by-stage reading of the ceiling.

The forcefulness of the painted figures relegates the simulated architecture into the background. Their dynamism is such that any question as to the verisimilitude of the architectural framework is passed over. Yet it is out of that framework that arises the subtle, ambiguous and polyvalent relation between the different "realities" of this Mannerist decoration.

The Pauline Room in the Castel Sant'Angelo was painted by Perin del Vaga and Pellegrino Tibaldi for the greater glory of Pope Paul III, the former Cardinal Alessandro Farnese.[33] The frescoed walls illustrate the deeds of Alexander the Great; medallions over the doors evoke the life of St Paul; the theological and cardinal virtues, together with an imposing archangel Michael, complete the whole, whose interpretation raises no problems. At that crucial moment—on the eve of the Council of Trent where Reformation and Counter-Reformation confronted each other—the pope as all-powerful arbiter wished to keep the balance between classical culture and Christian spirituality. The harmony of the decoration stems precisely from the agreement between this complex iconography and the painted architectonic side-scenes. It was an agreement through disagreement, for the fresco takes over the contradictions and tensions underlying the iconography. Indeed, as in Peruzzi's Hall of Perspectives, the principal articulation of the painted architecture is created by the columns. But while in the Farnesina they support the entire decoration of the room, here, though taken singly they have the density of an actual building element, these columns taken in their entirety seem flattened out in relation to the wall. But which wall? The question arises because the space beyond the columns does not reveal its structure. They serve to support the stucco cornice of the room, and their capitals stand at the very limits of the real space. Yet the columns should logically move back in order to give place to the winged creatures in the foreground. So that here, curiously enough, one is thrown back into a medieval space, comparable to that of Duccio's *Maestà*, where the spatial effect is obtained by the superimposed planes of the decoration, without any attempt to achieve an internal coherence.[34] The purpose of the architectural element is overlooked, and its verisimilitude is fragmentary. Confronted by these iconographic and conceptual contradictions, one wonders what meaning to attach to the figure of the servant with a muscular torso, hurrying away through the sham door opening on a non-existent staircase. The latter is in fact the exact replica of the real one which, in the "Pompeian Corridor," forms a pendant to it.[35]

More explicit still is the praise voiced by Vasari for Pope Paul III, in which the painter relates "the stories and deeds of Pope Paul III, and in each his portrait from life." And there indeed is the pope, with his Ti-

Giorgio Vasari (1511-1574):
Hall of the Hundred Days,
Palazzo della Cancelleria, Rome.
1546.

◁ Perin del Vaga (c. 1501-1547)
and
Pellegrino Tibaldi (1527-1596):
Sala Paolina or Council Hall,
Castel Sant'Angelo, Rome.
1546-1547.

tianesque profile, distributing honours to "reward virtue, handing out knighthoods, benefices, pensions, bishoprics and cardinals' caps. Among the personages receiving them, Sadoleto, Polo, Bembo, Contarino, Giovio and Buonarroti and other great men, all portrayed from life... Envy is there too, eating vipers, and appears to choke on the venom."[36] In the words of a contemporary, "they were all dressed in a manner anciently modern and modernly ancient."[37] Contradictory like this judgment of it, the organization of the painting is discontinuous, the forms sinuous; scale changes suddenly from one plane to the next, reality is mixed with illusion, and truth with alle-

gory. Here then once more is the world of contrasts and tensions typical of Mannerism. It is a world which the spectator is urged to enter, by way of an elegant staircase, a new invention of which the painter shows himself very proud. Convex at first, then concave, and bathed in a lunar light, this staircase seems real. One's puzzlement lasts only a moment, however, for like the figures represented at the top, the staircase is seen to have no space in which to unfold. Flattened against the wall, it is actually no more than a harmonious pattern of lines and surfaces. The ambiguity of this deceptive trompe-l'œil, this apparent but false reality, is spellbinding.

Francesco Salviati (1510-1563):
Palazzo Sacchetti, Rome.
1553-1554.

which leads her irresistibly to her lover. In view of the liberties taken both in the moral content of the fresco cycle (painted, after all, to the glory of a liberal churchman) and in the poetics of figural representation, one is tempted to look for a more coherent standpoint in the massive architecture which acts as support for the paintings. Above the dado rise gigantic columns to support the cornice. And here already one wonders: columns or pilasters? The full roundness suggests the presence of columns, the rectangular capitals contradict it. It would seem that there are two rows of columns, delimiting what is perhaps a loggia. Is it open or closed? The impenetrable dark of the background rules out any investigation. In the upper part one notes four capitals in front and four at the back. In the lower part there are only six. Where are the two missing columns? The heavy pictures are held by strips of light cloth, coiling capriciously round the columns. In this decoration, for all its imposing solidity, the laws of logic and gravity have been abolished. A whimsical and saturnine artist, taking advantage of the freedom left him by a liberal client, Salviati succeeded here in creating that "relation of uncertainty," that fascinating ambiguity which Vasari demanded of "modern" art: "A freedom which, while outside the rules, was guided by them, and which was not incompatible with order and correctness. This called for a prolific invention and the beauty of the smallest details."[39]

The great hall of the Palazzo Sacchetti was decorated for Cardinal Ricci by Salviati with scenes from the life of David.[38] The churchman who had been a young secretary from Montepulciano, and became in Rome a possible pope, chose the story of the Old Testament hero who, from a shepherd, became a king. The analogy between the two destinies is too obvious to be accidental.

One wall in the room illustrates the story of David's connection with Bathsheba, the sole episode in the king's life in which he proved guilty. Yet the cardinal and his artist did not elude the subject. The story is set out on the wall in three scenes. In the centre, Bathsheba at her bath, unveiling her beauty to the king's eyes. On either side, the consequences of this indiscretion: on the left, the slaying of Uriah, her husband, and on the right, Bathsheba going up for her union with David. This layout, presented as if on a processional banner, is one of the finest successes of Mannerist painting. The turning figure of Bathsheba is shown four times on the absurd winding staircase

Exteriors

The ephemeral decoration of an outside surface, painted façades are known to have existed from ancient times. Tacitus already refers to them, and there still exist some remains of polychromy imitating construction materials which date back to the early centuries of our era. The Gothic urban façade, of a faintly architectonic character, with an arrangement of openings dictated solely by the necessities of the interior, was sometimes adorned with a linear decoration which did no more than accentuate its unordered structure. In their most refined expression, the painted elements refer back to the work of the stone chiseller, who embellished windows with an added contour or embedded them in simulated lacework turrets.[40]

Renaissance architecture and its harmonious three-dimensional modulation completely changed the structure and role of the façade. Establishing contact with the outside world, it was given a character of representation and a didactic aspect. The building being designed to last, the need was felt to change the Gothic façade. The solutions adopted raised the problem—still crucial today—of the choice between imitation, adaptation or destruction of an outmoded past. In early sixteenth century Rome, some talented artists keenly interested in archaeology like Peruzzi and Polidoro da Caravaggio transformed the city into a sumptuous but temporary stage-set. Using the technique of *sgraffito* (scratchwork) and grisaille, they punctuated the façades with elements of painted architecture which permitted them to introduce the classical order and symmetry, but also to make the most of a decoration with niches containing statues or friezes in high relief.[41]

This answered of course to an aesthetic need, but it was also a rapid solution which satisfied the pressing demands of a clientele of *nouveaux riches* who had come to Rome in successive waves, attracted by the entourage of the popes.

Giacomo Ripanda (15th century):
Courtyard vault, Castle of Civita Castellana (Viterbo).
Scratch-work and grisaille.
About 1500.

Polidoro da Caravaggio
(1495/1500-1546):
Façade, Palazzo Gaddi
(demolished), Rome.

47

Perin del Vaga (c. 1501-1547):
Decorative design for the north front,
Palazzo Doria, Genoa.

Triumphal pageantry and holiday façades could transform a city during the visit of some illustrious personage. Thus Vasari relates how, in honour of the pope's visit in November 1515, Florence was turned into an imperial Rome for only 5,000 florins. For the occasion, Andrea del Sarto and Jacopo Sansovino created a wooden façade painted in grisaille to cover the front of the cathedral, which was designed "in a German style and order": the temporary façade was much admired by the pope, who considered "that it could not have been finer even had it been made of marble."[42]

Yet, as the works of Titian and Giorgione in Venice testify,[43] these painted façades were sometimes more than an economical device for draping "Gothic bodies in modern clothing"[44] for a brief period.

Made to be applied to the denuded surface of the suburban villa of the Dorias, the design by Perin del Vaga is much more than a mere architectural adjustment. As the wall surface in contact with public life, this north façade was meant to be representative of the palace and its master. The use of rustic work on the basement and for the powerful columns was a revolutionary step at that time.[45] Advocated by the theorist Serlio, after the example of antiquity, as a symbolic token of force in the work of nature, it was to be one of the strong points of the coming architectural ideology of Mannerism.[46] Rustication was thus an integral part of the conceptual significance of the villa-palace. In the image of Camillus, the early sa-

viour of Rome (whose story is depicted in simulated bas-reliefs in the upper order of the façade), Andrea Doria wanted himself to be seen as robust and stern, generous and heroic, a new "Father of his Country."[47] The façade painted in trompe-l'œil could thus act as both a political and artistic manifesto.

In the North, where Gothic was more firmly rooted, the confrontation of the two worlds resulted in a sharp crisis and hybrid solutions. To celebrate the transit of the Emperor Maximilian I at Trento and to renovate a large house in the centre of the town, an artist designed a façade which, in a distinctively Germanic way, attempted to adapt the "modern" style to a medieval decoration.[48] Thus creating a half real, half fictive space, the painter divided the façade into horizontal strips by varying the decoration of the surface: in the lower part, it imitates a marble facing; in the upper, the pattern of a fabric. The windows are framed and emphasized by pillars in perspective. In the upper part beneath the roof, the emperor and his retinue are represented leaning over the balcony balustrade adorned with rugs, and looking down into the street. This colourful scene, though still medieval, remains plausible. In the *piano nobile*, on the other hand, without any logic, the wall is dissolved and gives place to a patron St George, riding through nature. Another scene, further on, shows an inner room full of people. An incongruous solution but undeniably a pictorial one, for the back wall of this room opens in turn and the sky can be seen through a window.

Palazzo Geremia, Trento,
North Italy.
Early 16th century.

It was probably a heresy of this kind that Serlio condemned, for "it is not advisable for a façade to contain any opening such as imitates the atmosphere or landscape; these things break up a building and change a compact and solid form into a transparent one, without any firmness, like that of an imperfect or ruined building."[49]

More coherent and sophisticated was the solution adopted by the Grand Duke Ferdinand II of Tyrol to renovate, in the taste of his day, the façade of the inner courtyard of the castle of Ambras.[50] As soon as he took possession of this fortress in 1563, he enlarged it and transformed it into a princely residence. But to make the old building acceptable, this prince whom

Heinrich Teufel (died 1570):
Inner courtyard, Castle of Ambras
(Innsbruck), Austria.
1567-1568.

Hans Bock the Elder (c. 1550/1552-1624):
Façade design.
1571.

appears to have been built around a central atrium, whereas in fact it had the solidity of a massive block. Two tiered towers advance aggressively into the space on the street side. These are disturbing constructions which recall both Babylon and Rome. But they answer the purpose of restoring symmetry to an incoherent façade still wholly Gothic in conception.[53] By means of a subtle visual device, the artist merges this irregularity of design into the perspective distortion due to the off-centre viewpoint which he has chosen. Making play with space and practising intellectual mystification, the Mannerism of this approach was apparently not much followed, but today it strikes us as highly imaginative and attractive.

The renewal of interest in archaeology, the use of the painted façade as an illustration of pagan mythology and, above all, its symbolism which extolled the cult of personality—all this the Counter-Reformation put an end to. As can also be seen from the drawings Rubens made from the façades he saw in Genoa, the trompe-l'œil now reverted to a purely architectonic role. It corrected medieval assymmetries, emphasized the articulations of the buildings and, on the urban level, now unified disparate buildings.[54] The requirements laid down by Serlio were then, and for a long time to come, entirely satisfied, "for by acting in this way one does not disrupt the order, one proceeds to paint reality and reinforce the decoration."[55]

Montaigne calls "the great builder" resorted to trompe-l'œil painting. A smooth nailhead rustication sets the tonality of the decoration. Simulated windows are inserted among the real ones in order to re-establish a harmonious rhythm.

Friezes in low relief represent mythological subjects. With the rows of niches housing statues, they testify to the humanistic culture of the castle's inhabitants. The existence of empty niches indicates that Ferdinand was familiar with what was then believed to be a feature of ancient architecture.[51] Furthermore, with a typically Germanic taste for colour and picturesqueness, birds and bouquets of flowers animate the simulated half-open windows. Evoking the luminous splendours of a Florentine Renaissance, the painted façade at Ambras recalls the personality of the prince, a cultivated ruler, but one closely attached to his native soil.

The façade designed by Hans Bock for the humanist Theodor Zwinger deepens the discrepancy between the actual and the simulated architecture. It places the latter on a quite different plane.[52] Here the house

Peter Paul Rubens (1577-1640):
Drawing of the façade, Palazzo Salvago, Genoa.

3

The Sacred Space

To integrate the past into the present, to magnify the room space and give it an opulence that could not otherwise be afforded, these were the motives behind the trompe-l'œil painting of architecture. The Church made ample use of them as a means of bringing before the faithful a continually renewed image of its power and wealth. Such paintings could also go much further, for by breaking down material barriers and transcending the limitations of matter this simulated architecture opened channels of communication between the divine and the earthly, turning the unreal into reality and transposing the real into vision.

Amplification

To embellish the House of God and give it the splendour that it deserves, by all available means, was always one of the prime concerns of the Church.

The Jesuits of Rome had long planned on crowning with a majestic dome the church they had begun building in Rome in 1627. But from lack of funds, and under pressure from the neighbouring Dominicans who feared that their library would be overshadowed by such a dome, they were compelled to give up the project. A painter, Father Andrea Pozzo, was accordingly called in, and on the bare ceiling over which it was supposed to have risen, he was commissioned to paint a dome which would amplify the church to the monumental dimensions desired.[1] Painted on canvas and then applied to the ceiling, it provoked criticism and controversy from the beginning, even though much admired as an ingenious piece of work. By the evocative power of contrasting lights and the imitation of a structure rightly considered impracticable by contemporary architects, Pozzo builds up a system of treble monumental columns resting on frail brackets. The columns support the coffered ceiling and delimit a gallery that extends round the drum of the dome. Windows, round-windows and lantern-turret provide the sources of light for this construction

strongly influenced by Bernini. An accomplished theorist of perspective, Pozzo explained in his treatise how he contrived this simulated dome. Built up by means of an external vanishing point, it has its roots in the "openings" of the Albertis and Tassi. However, in the complex decoration of the church of Sant'Ignazio and by virtue of its position in the crossing, it represents much more than the expression of a theorist's virtuosity. Thanks to its asymmetrical structure, it imposes a viewpoint beyond which the construction becomes absurd, even menacing. It accordingly points out to the worshipper, with authority, the place where he should stop in his advance through the church. Thus Pozzo's dome assumes a liturgical role, for, with no ambiguity for the layman, it indicates the limits of the approach permitted him.

An important element for the perception of space, the simulated dome may also have an iconological content. Indeed, from the beginnings of Christianity, the dome as substitute and image of the celestial vault symbolized the *Ecclesia*. In the elegant mortuary chapel of the Counts of Schönborn in Franconia, the painter Giovanni Francesco Marchini assigns this

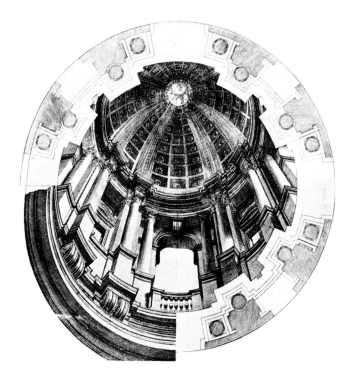

Andrea Pozzo (1642-1709):

◁ Church of Sant'Ignazio, Rome.
1685.

▽ ◁ Dome of the Collegio Romano, Rome.
From *Perspectiva pictorum et architectorum*, Rome, 1737.

▷ Giovanni Francesco Marchini (early 18th century):
Holy Cross Chapel, Church of Sankt Jakob,
Wiesentheid, Franconia.
1730.

profound significance to it.[2] If he enters the chapel by the north arm of the cross which contains the central octagonal space, the eyes of the worshipper are drawn upwards to a variant of Pozzo's dome. Surrounded in the pendentives by medallions representing the Instruments of the Passion, this dome recalls the Redemption through Christ. A carved group over the altar, in the centre of the chapel, represents the Crucifixion. Its soaring monumental verticalism carries the eye up to the vault where it glimpses another off-centre dome, with a balustraded gallery. Only as one approaches the altar does one become aware of the cataclysm which is about to bring down the huge blocks of stone. The Last Judgment seems to have arrived. The presence in the gallery of figures in the costume of the Reformed Church or in Eastern dress informs the worshipper that the Church being destroyed by the divine wrath is that of the heretics. It is the *Vera Ecclesia*, the Church of the Redemption, which welcomes the worshipper who has entered here. As eloquent as a historiated fresco, the simulated architecture of these two domes conveys a powerful spiritual message.

⊲ Cosmas Damian Asam (1686-1739):
Descent of the Holy Ghost in the
Abbey Church of St Martin and St Oswald,
Weingarten, Baden-Württemberg.
1718.

Cosmas Damian Asam (1686-1739):
Descent of the Holy Ghost in the
former Abbey Church of the Assumption of
the Virgin, St John the Baptist and St Ursula,
Aldersbach (Passau), Bavaria.
1720.

Imitated over and over again, the dome of Father Pozzo was adopted in churches and palaces throughout Europe. It was used at least twenty times by the Asam brothers, who were active in Germany in the early eighteenth century.[3] In the abbey church at Weingarten, one finds again the brackets, here monumental, which support the porticoes in order to constitute a fore-stage. A row of columns and pillars carry the coffered dome whose round-window lets in the light of the Holy Spirit. The foreshortening, more powerful than that of the original model, hides the architectonic details of the gallery and thus contributes to put the accent on the scene there taking place. The Virgin and apostles, together with a crowd

of witnesses, have taken their place in the narrow corridor assigned to them. Without belonging to the celestial world, this inhabited space does not belong to the church either. Uncertainty prevails.

A few years later, at Aldersbach, we find a hybrid assemblage of two domes. That of Father Pozzo is miniaturized and, as if symbolically, takes the place of the sky-light turret. The main dome has become huge and rests on columns devoid of any organic connection with the architecture of the church. A gilt stucco cornice clearly indicates the frontier. Solidly installed in front of this architecture, the saintly figures have the benefit now of a space of their own which they dominate. So it is that, overhead, a parallel world is

Antonio Galli Bibiena (1700-1774):
Chapel of the Holy Sacrament, Church
of the Assunta, Sabbioneta (Mantua).
1773.

created, glowing with colour, at once weighty and near, resolutely separated and detached from the white space of the church.

These two domes are in fact paradigmatic of the shift which, in the Germanic lands, thrust back simulated architecture from their world, which was meant to be real, into the world of illusion whose decor that architecture created.

While in the North these painted domes became a material but distant background, in Italy they gradually lost their architectural solidity. Often placed without any structural logic, and treated as a linear decor, they came to signify no more than an arabesque or a floral design.

Transformed into a pergola, the dome of Antonio Galli Bibiena has lost its materiality, and the chapel of the Holy Sacrament in the Assunta church at Sabbioneta, as thus amplified, finds its consummation in the vault of heaven.[4] With this total opening on the infinite, the Piedmontese stage-designer seems to close here the history of the cycle of the painted dome.

Transcendence

Church walls in the Middle Ages had been the "Bible of the Poor": there sacred history was pictured in eloquent ideograms. Incited by the accusations and repudiations of the Reformation, by the inroads of heretical doctrines, by the need to spread the Christian faith in pagan lands, and also perhaps in reaction against the austerity of the Counter-Reformation, the Church again resorted to the image as a powerful means of communication and propaganda. By opening up church vaults with trompe-l'œil paintings, it made the infinite visually accessible. Contact with the godhead was thus established and the glory of the saints affirmed the legitimacy of the Church's mission. The architecture of the new churches of the seventeenth century in Rome did not easily lend itself to the layout of the illusionist architecture which decorated the ceiling of secular buildings. On the one hand, the "avant-garde" architecture of a Bernini or a Cortona

Domenico Maria Canuti (1620-1684)
and
Enrico Haffner (1640-1702):
Glory of St Dominic in the Church of
SS. Domenico e Sisto, Rome.
1674.

ENTRANCE

CHOIR

was self-sufficing; on the other, the existence in the older churches of cross-ribs supporting the great vaults would have broken up the picture space and called rather for ceiling decorations made up of many *quadri riportati*.[5] Yet the latter half of the seventeenth century saw the creation of three works which did open up the vault and give access to the aerial heights of heaven.

In the church of Gesù in Rome, without using any framework of painted architecture, Giovan Battista Gaulli brought down a host of heavenly creatures into the church, and some of the figures overlap and cover the stucco mouldings. The sense of distance and depth is conveyed solely by the skilful play of lights and shadows. Yet this masterpiece by Gaulli got a cool welcome from his contemporaries. In the Barberini manuscript under date of 10 April 1675 we read: "Many were the connoisseurs who had no particular praise either for the intention [of Cavaliere Bernini] or for the work [of Baccici the Florentine]."[6]

Four months later, on 10 August 1675, we find this entry in the Barberini manuscript: "Monday the feast day of St Dominic was celebrated by the nuns of Montemagnapoli, and in their church was unveiled the very fine painted vault." Here then was another decoration which, in this case, won the approbation of contemporary critics. Working in the small Roman church of SS. Domenico e Sisto, the Bolognese painters Domenico Maria Canuti and Enrico Haffner covered the whole central part of the vault, opening up a view of the apotheosis of the patron saint. The penetrations of the median windows stand out against the sky, and those of the side windows are connected by two broad cross-ribs decorated with bas-reliefs in chiaroscuro. An architectural framework is thus created, bordered by an elegantly undulating balustrade, and its optical plane is only slightly detached from the real surface of the ceiling. The central perspective of this architecture without depth produces no visual tension for the spectator's eye. A luminous haze establishes the diffuse distance between earth and heaven, where St Dominic is ascending in glory. Fruit, flowers, volutes and angels contribute to the amiable, festive atmosphere which seems to have been very much to the taste of both the nuns and the Roman public.

CHOIR

▷ Johann Michael Rottmayr (1654-1730)
and
Gaetano Fanti (1687-1759):
Glory of St Benedict, Benedictine
Abbey Church, Melk, Austria.
1720-1721.

Fourteen years later, it was another force and another dimension that the Jesuits required for the church dedicated to their patron saint. "The idea of painting the entire vault was due to the extraordinary reputation acquired in painting the dome, not only by Father Andrea the artist but also by the Company that commissioned it... This vault painting was the greatest task that an artist could undertake," wrote Filippo Baldinucci.[7] And in 1688, overcoming all opposition, Andrea Pozzo stripped away the stuccoes adorning the vault, and taking no account of the latter he proceeded to cover it with the boldest architectural painting ever executed. Flawlessly linked up, register by register, with the real architecture, painted brackets, pillars and arcades go to form the dizzying open construction which soars up heavenwards. Built up in

accordance with all the rules of art, "con ottima regola," this vault painting has a rigorously central vanishing point.[8] Deriving from the school of Lombard quadraturisti, the suggested space seems to narrow down in order to focus the eye on the aerial heights where the grandiose spectacle of the glory of St Ignatius unfolds.

In a letter addressed to the Prince of Liechtenstein, Pozzo gives the key to the theme which he set out to illustrate. A quotation from St Luke defines the programme: "I am come to send fire on the earth; and what will I, if it be already kindled?"[9] It is the trajectory of that flame, spread through the world by the disciples of St Ignatius, that Father Pozzo delineated in his fresco. Though the artist has often been criticized for it, the perspective of the figures stretched out through the simulated architecture is not central, and each figure group is constructed with its own vanishing point.[10] But the discrepancy between the construction of the painted architecture and that of the figures is essential to the dynamic reading of the fresco. For Baroque space is an animated and spirited space which cannot be grasped by a static and passive attitude.

Having entered the church of Sant'Ignazio, the spectator is carried forward by the convergence of the architecture in trompe-l'œil to the centre of the church, where he is brought to a halt. Here, over this point of balance, is Christ bearing the Cross. The foreshortening of the body is coherent with that of the painted architecture; it marks in fact the centre of the world.[11] Receiving the light of the Father and the Holy Ghost, Christ becomes himself the source of light, one ray of which strikes St Ignatius, and the latter in turn directs it towards his disciples. From the Redeemer's heart emerges another ray which strikes a shield inscribed in incandescent letters with the monogram of Christ. If the worshipper leaves the central viewpoint and moves towards the altar to read the inscriptions, the height of the painted vault permits him to make this move without any risk of seeing the painted architecture fall out of balance. Yet the borderline of the permissible space is notified to him by the simulated off-centre dome which he feels as a barrier before him. It is when he turns round and walks along the walls that he understands the symbolic trajectory of the sacred fire which connects the disciples with the four continents of the world. He then perceives the figures in heavy, compact groups standing on the cornices and leaning towards the interior of the church. Finally, he will feel the menace of the huge, near-by figures of the unbelievers, gliding along the pilasters, driven in their inexorable downfall towards the darkness.

With its staggering upward soar, Father Pozzo's trompe-l'œil painting imparts an aggressive reality to the transcendence of the doctrine. At the same time, by means of a parallel movement, it makes its impact felt, while respecting the heavenly hierarchies and those of mortal men.

In the intentions behind them, the decorations painted in Germany and Austria during the seventeenth and eighteenth centuries are never very far from Italy, the native land of virtuoso illusionism. The Austrian Johann Michael Rottmayr, in collaboration with Gaetano Fanti, decorated the majestic abbey church of Melk in Austria with a fresco which recalls both the Bolognese type of *mise en scène* practised by Haffner and the grandiose conceptions of Father Pozzo.[12] The vault of the single nave at Melk rests on pilasters which delimit several bays. The ceiling of the church seems to have been removed, leaving only the cross-

ribs to support the vault. A low balustrade resting on the cross-ribs rises up heavenwards. Typically Bolognese in taste and style, it appears and disappears according to the whims of a Baroque sensibility. Yet it contributes to smooth away the divisions of the ceiling, and the worshipper's dynamic perception of it suggests the path he should follow to understand the iconography and to steep himself in the atmosphere of this sumptuous church. Thus the simulated architecture of each bay is best seen from a vanishing point

which precedes the bay.[13] In the first one, the saint represented in a forceful foreshortening has already arrived at the zenith of his heavenly ascension. Moving on to the second bay, one sees him again in a position which appears to be vertical in relation to the church of which he marks the centre. In the last bay, one's attention is focused on two monks who, from their sidelong position, are eyewitnesses of the saint's apotheosis. Though visually satisfying, the path punctuated with pauses which the spectator has had to follow is, from the conceptual point of view, the wrong approach. It is only by retracing his steps that he finally falls in with the logical sequence of the story depicted. Proceeding step by step, impelled forward now by the simulated architecture, he follows the gaze of the visionary monks and, led on by the angels who help him over the barriers of the vault soffits, accompanies St Benedict up to his final crowning.

The emperor, clergy and monks, on the other hand, as motionless spectators in the choir, had the benefit of the privileged orientation which gives them immediate access to the edifying spectacle of the apotheosis of the Church Militant.[14]

Thus in the inner space of the Melk church, as defined by the tremulous play of curves and countercurves, the worshipper, guided by the simulated architecture, is led to participate by his pendular approach in the tidal movement inherent in this late Baroque aesthetic.

The imaginary architecture that covered and "replaced" the church vaults permitted the pictorial expression of a mysticism based on the ascension towards the godhead. As against this, in the work of Bernardo Vittone, the real architecture and the simulated architecture come together and interlock in a more concrete and intellectual vision of the divine essence descending to earth to illuminate the world of mortal men. With Vittone, light is the expression of an act of grace, and its introduction into the church by means of an open architecture becomes the manifestation of a cult. The creator, if not the inventor, of countless pierced vaults, opened-up pendentives and luminous round-windows, he sought this light in spaces hidden from the eyes of the faithful. Double calottes and upper galleries with invisible windows thus became a source of radiance. This was in fact the same mysterious light coming from a "beyond" which simulated architecture had brought into the space which it decorated. So it is that, with Vittone, we often find this interaction between actual and simulated architecture. In his work, illusion inspires or replaces reality.

The church of San Bernardino at Chieri stands under the sign of the radiant monogram of Christ as revealed and propagated by the saint. In this church, the sun in its daily course through the sky successively illuminates the hidden spaces surrounding the vault. The perforated pendentives of the dome, adorned with radiating fasces in stucco, diffuse the light which floods the space with a subdued brightness. Steeped in this at once mystical and Newtonian vision of light, which materializes after being reflected by successive obstacles, Vittone reverted to it again and again, almost obsessively.[15] He went so far as to introduce it, by various subterfuges, in the modest churches where its material realization was out of the question. It is his will and his conception, then, that one recognizes in the work of the mediocre painter who executed the trompe-l'œil decoration of his church at Riva di Chieri. Here the vase of flowers, seen in back-lighting in the non-existent opening of a pendentive, plays the same role as the stucco decoration in the church of San Bernardino.[16] Thus the architect, as both creator and builder, himself chose the painted architecture designed to express a fundamental postulate of his conception of space.

Vittone can undoubtedly be credited with the novel idea of using the perforations of the dome to illuminate paintings executed on a second shell external to it. It is possible, however, that he found this solution in a painted decoration done in trompe-l'œil.[17] For the structure of the church of Santa Chiara at Brà reappears in the simulated architecture painted some ten years before at Stupinigi, under the watchful eye of the great architect Filippo Juvara.[18] At Santa Chiara,

Bernardo Vittone (1705-1770):
◁◁ Church of San Bernardino, Chieri, Piedmont.
1740-1744.

◁ Painted decoration, Church of the Assunta, Riva di Chieri, Piedmont.
1766-1767.

▷ Filippo Juvara (1676-1736):
Painted decoration by the Valeriani brothers,
Hunting Lodge,
Stupinigi, Piedmont.
1733.

▽ Bernardo Vittone (1705-1770):
Church of Santa Chiara,
Brà, Piedmont.
1742.

Gian Domenico Rossi (active 1755-1763):
Church of the Confraternità della Misericordia, Saluzzo, Piedmont.
1763.

as Vittone himself writes, "the upper vault paintings meeting your eye as you stand in the church, thanks to the light supplied by the dormer-windows surrounding them," embody the vision of his precursor and *maître à penser*, who, for his part, had contented himself with a trompe-l'œil substitute.[19]

So it was in the framework of late Piedmontese Baroque, as represented by such great architects as Guarini, Juvara and Vittone, that this "luminism" of the presence of God had been materialized. This was also the moment when trompe-l'œil found itself cast in a new role. Without fundamentally modifying the actual space, it became a device utilized by the architect himself, in parallel with his architectural work, to make everywhere present the light of transcendence. The lightness and transparency of the open architec-

ture made it possible for architectural trompe-l'œil to achieve that total fusion between reality and illusion which sometimes smoothes the approach to spirituality. Taking up the invention of the architect Vittone, the simulated dome of the church of the Confraternità della Misericordia at Saluzzo appears to have a double calotte. The coffered vault can just be made out in the background. The presence of the Holy Ghost, descending from heaven through the central round-window, illuminates the vault and seems to dissolve it in the atmosphere. The ceiling is transformed into lacework and a divine light floods the church. Light and transparent, with its incurving balustrades and perforated pendentives, this luminous diaphragm takes over in the church the role of the stained-glass window.

Humanization

As a mirror of reality, the simulated architecture creates a setting very close at hand in which the mysteries of Holy Scripture can be pictured. The worshipper need make no effort to move out of his own world and imagine another. He is not required to overstep the limits of the architecture surrounding him in order to gain access to the infinity of the godhead. Now, on the contrary, the inhabitants of the celestial spheres and the actors of sacred history are living and close: they come to him, sharing his space in a nearness that trompe-l'œil makes very real.

The "new Jerusalem" built by Friar Bernardino on the hills of Varallo answered at the same time to the wave of fervour aroused by the Franciscans and to the dangers of heresy coming from northern Europe. The multiplication of the stations of self-communion offered the pilgrim not only a place of prayer but also the possibility of identifying himself with the three-dimensional world, colourful, animated and lifelike, of Christ's Passion.[20] Every device was resorted to in order to create this arresting ensemble. The painted architecture is enhanced with reliefs, and lifesize figures in wood or coloured stucco wear "modern" clothing, some of it made of real materials. Beards and hair made of horsehair adorn their faces. The wicked are repulsively ugly, the good and honest handsome and appealing, no excess being spared in these scenarios in which architecture, sculpture and painting intermingle. The aim was to create a spectacle exceeding in intensity all that the *sacre rappresentazioni* could evoke here and now. Expressionism and hyperrealism seem to have been invented here. Wrought-iron screens were set up in order to separate reality from illusion. Yet, once he has applied his eye to the opening provided for him, the worshipper is spellbound. There he participates fully in a sacred history humanized and transposed into his own present.

Il Morazzone (c. 1571-1626)
and
Tanzio da Varallo (1576-c. 1655):
Ecce Homo Chapel, Church of Sacro
Monte, Varallo, Piedmont.
1609.

Giulio Benso (1601-1668):
Annunciation, Church of the Santissima
Annunziata del Vastato, Genoa.
1638.

Far from her humble home in Nazareth, the Virgin
Mary is visited by the angel Gabriel. She is seen leaning on a balustrade in an upper gallery of the church
of the Santissima Annunziata del Vastato in Genoa.
The simulated architecture surrounding her with a
majestic wealth of gilded forms can in no way be dis-
tinguished from the actual architecture. The line of
demarcation between the real and the imaginary has
been completely effaced, and the worshipper becomes the privileged witness of the mystery of
Christ's conception. So forcible is this evocation that
it conveys the certainty of actual experience. It is
moreover as much a theological statement as a political manifesto. The glorification of the Virgin had a
long iconographical tradition behind it. What it sig-
nified first of all was obedience to the Roman Church
in its struggle against the Reformation. The accession
of the Republic of Genoa to the ''Titolo Regio'' in the
name of ''Maria Santissima'' corresponded to an affir-
mation of its might as a sea-power and seaport rein-
vigorated by a prestigious renewal of prosperity. The

Virgin of the Annunciation becomes the Virgin Queen.[21] Her house is the place of glory that she shares with all the inhabitants of the city. In the Genoa church, the architectural trompe-l'œil becomes a supporting structure. It is the essential, driving element behind the visual transmission of the concept.

The corridor connecting the rooms in which St Ignatius of Loyola lived till his death was decorated a century later by Father Pozzo. Along the walls, surrounded by simulated architecture, unfold the scenes of the saint's life.[22] The fictive space is skilfully linked up with the real, by a virtuoso hand. Ornaments, curtains, columns and capitals, nothing of this is real. At the end of the corridor is a podium framed by simulated columns where a concert is taking place. The divine music is executed by angels who have come down from heaven to celebrate the glory of St Ignatius. By humanizing the celestial creatures, the simulated architecture gives them a place in the world of mortal men. The sanctified founder of the Jesuits, on the other hand, is present only *in effigie*: removed into non-reality, his icon-portrait is in fact the trompe-l'œil of a picture.

Here, though it is supposed to be the specular image of reality, the trompe-l'œil nonetheless weaves the plot of a dumb show in which the roles are reversed.

Andrea Pozzo (1642-1709):
Corridor of St Ignatius' rooms,
Collegio Romano, Rome.
1682-1686.

Charles Natoire (1700-1777),
Gaetano Brunetti (died 1758),
Paolo Antonio Brunetti (1723-1783):
Chapel of the Foundling Hospital, Paris.
1751.
Print by Etienne Fessard after
Augustin de Saint-Aubin.

The chapel (now demolished) of the Foundling Hospital in Paris was at once a basilica and a cottage.[23] Thanks to the inventiveness of Charles Natoire, it became the very place of Christ's birth. Executed with extreme finesse, the simulated architectural structure opens the space on two levels. The separation of the interior is obtained, in the lower register, by means of an arcade standing on elegant pillars with Ionic and Doric colonnettes. The upper part takes over the same rhythm; it is supported, however, by rustic-work masonry and shows unmistakable signs of dilapidation. Finally, the imaginary space finds its crowning-piece in the sky overhead, from which it is separated by the remains of a coffered ceiling in ruins. On the outer side of the arcade, the retinue of the Magi on the one hand and groups of shepherds on the other are moving towards the centre. In the upper gallery, facing the windows, nuns and orphans lean on the balustrades and watch the scene.

Surrounding the spectator and sweeping him up, the architecture and figures thus converge on the altar. The borderline between story and reality, between past and present, is abolished in order that the worshipper may participate directly in the adoration of the Magi. It was for all, in a dazzling play of light, that "the multitude of the heavenly host praised God."[24]

Reproduced in prints and distributed to illustrious clients, the decoration of Natoire and the Brunettis met with an immediate and resounding success.[25] One can understand its popularity, for this work illustrates exceptionally well the growing taste for the representation of ruins. Moreover, the artists skilfully reverted to an iconographical tradition which had been long forgotten. The birth of Christ marks the precise moment of the transition from the age *sub lege* (under the law of Moses) to the age *sub gratia* (under the grace of the Redeemer). The simulated architecture of the building subtly conveys this antithesis between the Old and the New Testament, between the ruins of the past and the splendour of the present. The architectural trompe-l'œil of the Brunettis thus plays a dual role. Humanizing sacred history, it imparts to it a compelling reality and immediacy. It situates the episode at a precise moment and gives it the dimension of its timeless implications.

Sebastiano Serlio (1475-1554):
Tragic Scene, stage design.
Woodcut from his *Libro primo...
d'architettura*, Venice, 1551.

4
The Ludic Space

Play-acting and make-believe, living in an imaginary environment or watching others do so, these were so many ludic activities for which the architectural trompe-l'œil could provide the setting. The playhouse organized, conditioned and "staged" this escape mechanism for a passive and receptive spectator. By means of factitious scenery, it created for the actors a plausible world, external to the real world of the spectator. When the inhabited space of everyday life is transformed by simulated architecture, it becomes a theatrical space which calls for and makes possible the ludic activity of spectators now converted into actors. So it is, very often, that fictive characters take over and, concealed or displayed within the painted architecture, they become the audience of a living show.

The framework of this festival scenery may be permanent. It then gives the cue for the play-acting and strikes up like music, as soon as one enters. It accompanies the visitor up the grand staircases and down the corridors to the ballroom, the epicentre of the festivities. The illusion may be strong enough to abolish the walls and carry the pageant into the gardens. Opening windows or closing doors, trompe-l'œil may facilitate this evasion, just as it may hinder and prohibit it.

The theatre space

Wall paintings of simulated architecture have always had stage scenery as their backdrop and term of comparison. In both cases the intentions and effects are the same, for the purpose of both is to create a fictive environment acting on the spectator and transposing him into an imaginary world. The stage scenery simulates the setting of an action which is played out before a motionless audience regrouped in front of the scene. Mobile and ephemeral, it offers, in one and the same spectacle, a series of sites grafted on to the unchanging data of a frontal or oblique view. As against this, the *quadratura* is a permanent and

immutable setting for a moving spectator: it calls for a variety of points of view. Owing to these fundamental differences between them, the two genres have evolved on lines of their own. Yet their affinities are undeniable, for they rely on the same technical procedures deriving from the assumptions of perspective. So it is no accident if the great *quadraturisti* are periodically found to reveal themselves as skilful scene painters. Thus the central perspective of Peruzzi and Serlio, as well as the diagonal views of the Bibienas, undoubtedly found an echo in the trompe-l'œil architectural frescoes on religious and secular themes.

The theatrical aspect was not limited however to the stage space. To enact the pageantry required from painter and spectator a state of mind permitting them to overstep the boundaries of everyday reality and enter a transformed or imaginary world. This festival mood had to be induced and maintained by the theatrical setting.

Giuseppe Galli Bibiena (1696-1756):
Setting for the Theatrum Sacrum of
the Court Chapel in Vienna.
1740.

Costanzo Arbaudi (died 1657)
and
Francesco Arbaudi (died after 1661):
Courtyard, Castle of Maresco, near Saluzzo (Piedmont).
1613-1623.

Vincenzo Scamozzi (1552-1616):
Olympic Theatre, Sabbioneta
(Mantua).
1588.

With this purpose in mind, the ancients had built theatres in which stage and auditorium were designed in relation to each other in order to create the setting necessary to remove actor and spectator from their usual surroundings. In the Middle Ages, on the other hand, plays were enacted in public squares and churches fitted up for the occasion. Ingenious and complicated, these performances called for a dynamic participation on the part of the spectator, who had to take in, one after another, the multiple fictive spaces aligned before his eyes.[1] Secular pageants, carnivals and political events afforded an opportunity of creating imaginary environments and stage devices. Then the show became general, it was not confined to any particular place, and the aspect of the city was temporarily changed by a "speaking" architecture.[2] Thus in the sixteenth century the perspective of the street was modified by triumphs and by receptions of the ruler; tilting matches transformed the public squares and comedies animated the palace courtyards.

The frescoes adorning the inner courtyard of Maresco Castle in Piedmont testify, still today, to the organization of a *cortile* as a theatre space.[3] The spectators, being absent, are only evoked by the presence of sim-

ulated statues in niches and by busts on the pediments: the display was executed for the entertainment of the princes of Piedmont. The galleries, on the other hand, with their cross-ribbed vaults, are blithely peopled with figures. Picturesque characters in period costumes, playing instruments of that day, provide the background music for the fête in store. The trompe-l'œil evokes its overture.

When, as in antiquity, the theatre was sited in a definite place of its own, the decoration was given another scope. Yet the transformation of the theatre space still remains perceptible. Thus the amphitheatre of Vincenzo Scamozzi's Olympic Theatre at Sabbioneta is crowned with a porticoed loggia, and on top of it stand out, elegant and majestic, the statues of the gods of Olympus. The back wall takes over the same rhythm and simulated statues of the Roman emperors adorn non-existent niches. The prevailing tone of nobleness is accordingly set. On the upper level, however, a simulated gallery surrounds the amphitheatre and contains with difficulty a crowd of figures. These are the witnesses and spectators of the play-acting which is taking place both on the stage and in the auditorium.

Giambattista Tiepolo
(1696-1770)
and
Gerolamo Mengozzi-Colonna
(c. 1688-c. 1772):
Drawing-room,
Palazzo Labia, Venice.
1747-1750.

The scene of Cleopatra's repast and that of her meeting with Antony were painted by Tiepolo for the drawing-room of the Palazzo Labia in Venice. The artist created a world apart, luminous, remote, refined. It is an unreal, theatrical world, with scenes played for the benefit of spectators moving about the drawing-room. To this, the magnificence of the architectural structure painted in trompe-l'œil by Gerolamo Mengozzi-Colonna stands in contrast, by its weight, its volume, its grandiose materiality. Yet the architectural structure does not seem to have the three dimensions of a building, nor the slightest connection with the real wall. It is above all a *frons scaenae* in the antique manner, as described by Vitruvius. With its central arcade delimited by pillars, and surmounted by an upper storey patterned with pilaster strips and openings, this simulated architecture remains that of a partition-wall, a separation in back-lighting between the theatre space and the scene played.

To provide the Château de Condé-en-Brie with a theatre space, Giovanni Niccolò Servandoni transformed the reception room into a meeting place of actors and spectators, musicians and audience, all of them surrounded and isolated from the rest of the house by a unique setting. [4] For here, showing himself a talented stage designer, he covered the four walls with immense canvases painted in architectural trompe-l'œil. Stretched at a certain distance from the wall, they were intended to improve the acoustics and permit, when wanted, a quick change of scenery. This temporary arrangement proved permanent, and the canvases have remained in place for two centuries. A delicate pink monochrome colours the simulated marble pilasters that pattern the walls. Only a few accents of blue in the coffered ceiling and the frieze medallions go to break the monotony. In the niches, simulated statues of the continents accompany the goddesses of antiquity, forming a whole in which the figures and above all the inscriptions allude continually, and sometimes quite boldly, to the mythological loves of the gods. Over the mantelpiece, behind the sculptural group cut in outline, representing the rape of Proserpine, still stands the original mirror.[5] Though marked by the ravages of time, it multiplies *ad infinitum* the reflection of this fictive space, once given over to play-acting and entertainments.

Seeing and being seen

When transformed by an architectural trompe-l'œil, real space may in turn become a theatrical stage. Fictive characters, set out in the painted architecture, then become the attentive spectators of a dumb show enacted for their benefit.

The Sala Regia (Royal Hall), one of the most imposing rooms in the Quirinal palace in Rome, was in the early seventeenth century the Hall of the Consistory.[6] In the upper part, facing the real windows, simulated openings carry the eye towards some vaulted loggias standing in a fictive space much brighter and more aerial than that of the actual room. As a festival token, some precious rugs and brocades—painted of course —are draped over the balustrades which are barely sufficient to contain the host of spectators. Among them

Giovanni Niccolò Servandoni (1695-1766):
Drawing-room, Château of Condé-en-Brie (Aisne).
About 1740.

Agostino Tassi
(c. 1580-1644)
and
Giovanni Lanfranco
(1582-1647):
Sala Regia, Palazzo
del Quirinale, Rome.
1616-1617.

Charles Le Brun (1619-1690):
Grand Staircase or Escalier des
Ambassadeurs, Versailles.
1676-1678.
Print by Surugue.

are some ecclesiastics, but also many figures in Oriental costumes. Leaning out dangerously over the edge of the loggias, they seem intent on losing not one word of the performance taking place beneath their eyes. Tassi's painted architecture, done in drastic foreshortening, is constructed from several points of view, justified by the staggering height over which it extends. On the other hand, the spectators are represented in such a way as to benefit by the ideal viewpoint. Luminous and colourful, bearing witness to the activities of the Church militant, the new converts from distant countries are irresistibly present as leading spectators and actors.

Some sixty years later, in a design by Charles Le Brun, the same exotic and picturesque figures are shown looking over a simulated balustrade facing the grand staircase at Versailles.[7] Their curiosity is evident, but discreet enough not to ruffle their dignity. What are they gazing at from the top of these grandiose loggias in simulated precious marble? They are looking at their own doubles. They are gazing at the ambassadors, from the four quarters of the globe, who are mounting the steps leading to the apartments of the Sun King, Louis XIV.

Decked out in all his finery, a gentleman is preparing to enter the private audience chamber of the Grand Duke Ferdinando II de' Medici. At the bottom of the painted staircase, he is standing beside the painted column twined with gilded ivy. Self-importantly, he holds his decoration in one hand and his gloves in the other. The real space was only furnished with six fine chairs and a table.[8] In the privacy of the audience chamber, this gentleman's gaze probably meets that of the prince alone. They size each other up. Who is the actor, who the spectator, in this face-to-face encounter between reality and fiction?

Seeing and being seen: each tosses back the ball. The interplay of reflecting mirrors and virtual images is essential to trompe-l'œil. There lies all its charm.

Display and ostentation

In both princely dwellings and country seats, the decoration reflects the love of scenic play-acting and the pleasure of living in colourful, artificial surroundings. From the façade to the state rooms, spaces are multiplied and reality is enlarged, expanded, taking on a sumptuous magnificence. Let the festivities begin!
The carriage entrance and the owner's coat of arms welcome the visitor. The massive, vaulted porch leads him towards the flowered courtyard. The entrance to the château is marked by an elegant Baroque portico with double colonnade and projecting cornice.[9] Embellished with urns and surmounted by the emblematic figures of the Salenegg family, the portico of

their castle gives direct access to the entrance hall. It is made transparent and luminous by large bay-windows, while a staircase with wrought-iron banister points the way upwards. Yet everything here is illusion. In actual fact, to enter the building, one has to pass through an inner courtyard, hidden, severe and functional, that of a baronial hall which is also a country seat designed to accommodate the activities of a family of big wine-growers. The trompe-l'œil of the house front does, however, indicate the two facets of life at Salenegg castle: the cultivation of the land and the enjoyment of festivities. The owners hold open house; guests are always welcome.
Festivities take place on the *piano nobile*. This main floor, containing the reception rooms, is usually reached by stairs that are unimposing and rarely illuminated. It is here that the painted architecture takes

Salenegg Castle, Maienfeld, Grisons (Switzerland). 1782.

Pierre Daret (1604-1678):
Hôtel de Châteaurenard, Aix-en-Provence. 1654.

◁ Angelo Michele Colonna (1600-1687)
and
Agostino Mitelli (1609-1660):
Private Audience Chamber,
Palazzo Pitti, Florence.
1636-1641.

over. In the town house of Baron Châteaurenard at Aix-en-Provence, the architectonic novelties "burst out" conspicuously. Here one recognizes a deep-seated need to move back the walls and overcome the constraints of town life.[10] The conception of the staircase, built around a square core, is certainly new and indicates an attempt in provincial France to take over the design of a Parisian grand staircase. Here one meets that rare thing—ideal collaboration between an architect, Pierre Pavillon, and a painter, Pierre Daret. The result is a perfectly smooth extension of the built structure into a fictive space. The upward rise of the staircase ends on the first floor, and there the loggias painted in trompe-l'œil answer to the real balcony

A place of prestige and country residence, but also the centre of an extensive farm, the palatial villa of the local lords dominates a village near Brescia. It is a low building, but its compact design lends it a majestic serenity. One-third of the façade is heightened by a building unit which houses the ballroom. This unit is in fact the backbone and nerve centre of the whole. To reach it, one crosses an imposing porch followed by the *scala maestra*, a grand staircase of some width. The stairs lead into a gallery adorned with painted architecture—a Baroque surface decoration in a profuse and flowery style. It produces a sense of exhilaration: an irresistible *joie de vivre* prevails in this gallery, and here the festival mood is created. Through small internal windows, one divines the splendour of the drawing-room, suddenly revealed to the eye through a large central doorway. The visitor stands

rapt by this extraordinary space. Drawn out in a seemingly endless soar, the tower appears cylindrical, though one knows it to be rectangular. It is useless to try and divine the edges of the partitions. While the lesser walls retain the dainty structure of the *barocchetto* of the gallery painted by Giacomo Lecchi, the other two sides open broadly on to a dreamworld devised by Carlo Carlone. Here are enormous arcades, supported by clustered marble columns and framing two broad staircases which come to an end at our feet. On the steps stand the members of the family, gazing at us. The three children, at the top of the stairs, are silhouetted against the graceful colonnades of a garden pavilion designed in the style of an antique temple. Facing them, the master and mistress of the house, with their dog, are coming down with a light but resolute step. Servants here and there are going about their business. Behind them, in depth, extend the inner courtyards; they are connected by stairway banisters leading nowhere. Illogical and fascinating like the prisons of Piranesi or the stage scenery of the Bibienas, these side-scenes are bathed in a soft pinkish glow with golden overtones.[15]

Only little by little does one realize that the joy of the promised fête, one's initial impression, turns into uneasiness. Over the visitor comes a sense of being watched and belittled. Then, in the painted sky overhead, the eye meets the figures of Virtue, Reason, and History crowned by Fame. They observe you while the gods of Olympus are engaged in hurling the enemy forces of Obscurantism into the void. This brilliant cortège imposes its intellectual rigour. One is also seen and watched by the spectators seated in the side-boxes; and servants half concealed in the upper galleries also keep an eye on the visitor. But it is the presence of the master and mistress that makes the strongest impression. Larger than life, their imposing figures make one draw back in a space that has suddenly become exiguous. Why this subtle and elegant intimidation? Is it because the owner was not only a country gentleman but also and above all a high diplomat of the Venetian Republic charged with delicate arms transactions with the Emperor of Austria? Was he simply trying to amuse and impress the guests whom he housed in the mysterious non-communicating apartments in the wings of the castle?[16]

A place of entertainment and merry-making, the main drawing-room was also devoted to the cabals and intrigues which the master of the house conducted "at the peril of his life" but as an undisputed *deus ex machina*. The trompe-l'œil decoration thus contributed, visually and spiritually, to impose the owner's strong and interesting personality.

◁ ▷ Carlo Carlone (1686-1775),
Giacomo Lecchi and collaborators:
Drawing-room, villa near Brescia, North Italy.
1745.

A fantastic space, as full of movement and turnings as a saraband, the drawing-room of the Villa Crivelli near Milan comes as the quintessence of a game of prestidigitation.[17] The structure of the painted dado still rests solidly on the reality of the wall embellished with niches and plinths, but whose nature is respected. Suddenly the wall disappears, transformed into an undulating balustrade surmounted by strange aedicules with twisted marble columns, of an intense blue-green colour. Thus converted into a pavilion, the drawing-room opens towards an elegant inner courtyard surrounded by a severe, classical wall, of a gleaming whiteness. Transversal porticoes surmounted by powerful entablatures cut off the view, but show an immense sweep of sky where the drama of Phaethon is taking place. Among the figures, some are standing on the cornices and pediments; others are slipping behind the clouds. They accordingly mingle in the life of mortal men whose living space they share. A host of purely decorative elements go to embellish the view. On the balustrades are statues imitating bronze; vases, wreaths and baskets of flowers appear here and there, and monochrome reliefs adorn the overdoors.

Yet the painted architecture of the Galliari brothers always conveys the texture of the built elements; not only conveys it but magnifies it to the limits of plausibility. In this way it breaks down the set barriers of stage scenery constructed for spectators immobilized in a place external to them. The space it thus creates, while remaining strongly coordinated around a central focus, can be apprehended by a moving spectator from many points of view. In a specular play of repeated reflections, the kaleidoscope of painted architectures always remains coherent here. In the drawing-room of the Villa Crivelli, the artists have created a unique space, showy and exuberant, extravagant and prodigious in its inventiveness, yet always retaining the credibility of a dream.

Nearly forty years later, in the Château des Marches near Chambéry, the same Galliari brothers created a festival hall for a Savoyard castle-owner. The dream has dissolved, and the clear light of Reason takes its place. In this castle of the Marquis de Bellegarde reigns the logic of classicism, whose roots go back to the Renaissance. The ceiling, emphasized by coffers with painted rosettes, respects the volume of the built space. The living figures who once peopled the skies have disappeared, as if spellbound in the monumental monochrome of Olympian statues. With mathematical precision, the upper part of the room is divided in two, by means of a gallery running round it entirely. The balustrade, with its fine lacework of wrought-iron, is re-echoed in the fresco, where it has its exact counterpart. On the lower level, simulated banisters and pilasters alternate with medallions containing putti in grisaille. Above, between the large windows, the room is dominated by Diana and Minerva standing in painted niches. Behind the huge statues of Mars and Hercules, the secondary partitions are completely effaced. On one side appears a circular space, a pink and translucent pantheon crowned with a dome. It was apparently erected to the glory of the war god. Opposite, the point of infinity is plotted out, as in a treatise on architecture, by the bewildering and impossible perspective of a barrel vault. With its grey monochrome, faintly tinted with gold and pink, calm and majestic, the marquess's drawing-room is like an embodiment of the "Magnificent Place" sketched out in the past by the scene painter Giuseppe Galli Bibiena.

Bernardino Galliari (1707-1794)
and
Fabrizio Galliari (1709-1790):

◁ Drawing-room, Villa Crivelli,
Castellazzo di Bollate (Milan).
1752.

▽ Festival Hall, Château des Marches,
near Chambéry (Savoie).
1785-1790.

Giuseppe Galli Bibiena (1696-1756):
"Magnificent Place," sketch.
Early 18th century.

Antonio Galli Bibiena (1700-1774)
and collaborators:
Drawing-room, Casa Ferrari-Cartolari, Verona.
1765.

The work of Antonio Galli Bibiena and his collaborators, two simulated arcades framed by huge pilasters open up two facing walls in the drawing-room of the Ferrari-Cartolari house in Verona.[18] Through a painted gallery crowned with domes, the arcades lead the eye out towards illusory spaces confronting each other. In one, along an axis perpendicular to the wall, one crosses a courtyard and, by way of a gallery with multiple cross-vaults, ends up out of doors, under a blue sky. The other is a space parallel to the drawing-room, covered with a coffered barrel vault. The light bathing it seems to have effaced every trace of colour. The pictures representing ruins have become monochrome prints, and the floor tiling has lost its contrasting pattern. Observing a strictly central symmetry, two openings surmounted by pediments frame the statue of Minerva in her niche. The space thus opened up seems to be blind, dark and empty, like a mausoleum. Made up of elements which might belong to a tangible world, known and familiar, this plausible architecture nevertheless breaks off its connections with reality in order to create an abstract and metaphysical setting, such as might have been imagined later by a painter like Chirico. Is this bare, uninhabited and uninhabitable space still a make-believe or ludic space? It seems rather to sum up the contradictory mentalities of the period. For the eighteenth century was a crossroads of conflicting tendencies: on the one hand, a grandiloquent artistic past, vivid and colourful; on the other, a new Neo-classical current, representing a more rigid and schematized rationalism.

This was also the moment of time when the illusionist play of perspectives and volumes was losing ground. Scrolls, festoons and mouldings were flattened and multiplied. Stuccoes regained their place, and trompe-l'œil ennobled them with a factitious richness. The illusion was transformed into a pure and slavish decoration tied to the wall; the intervention of the artist lapsed into mere craftsmanship and tended towards anonymity. One thus observes a trend towards a fragmentation of painted architecture, depriving it of any weight and static content. As in the decoration painted by the Valeriani brothers for the hunting lodge of Stupinigi, the architectural trompe-l'œil may sometimes bewilder, but it ceases to deceive the eye.[19] Reaching here one of its limits, it shows itself ephemeral, occasional and showy, like a ball gown.

Filippo Juvara (1676-1736):
Painted decoration by the Valeriani brothers.
Hunting Lodge, Stupinigi, Piedmont.
1733.

Evasions

All barriers overthrown, the play of illusion traverses walls and extends into nature. The moralizing pretext had brought the landscape of the seasons into the inner room space, as a reminder of passing time. Now that pretext fell away, unthought of, and nature was present for its own sake, as a source of joy, an escape and evasion into unfamiliar surroundings.

Built as country residences, the villas of Frascati in the Alban Hills had from antiquity been seats of holiday pleasure for the well-to-do citizens of Rome. Surrounded by gardens, orchards and vineyards, these luxurious villas command still today a unique and spectacular view over the Roman Campagna. This panorama was known locally as the "theatre." So it was only natural to confront it with the "stage" of man-made gardens. [20]

The Hall of Spring in the Villa Falconieri at Frascati is wholly transformed into a garden by the trompe-l'œil fresco painted by Giovanni Francesco Grimaldi. From floor to ceiling, nature invades the room and invites the visitor to enter the undergrowth. The murmur of a real fountain seems to be echoed by the murmur of the leaves. The leafage of the trees, of many different kinds, conceals the articulation of the real walls and carries the eye towards distant temples and ruins. Here and there fragments of simulated architecture allude to the built element. These are in fact only so

Giovanni Francesco Grimaldi (1608-1680):
Hall of Spring, Villa Falconieri, Frascati (Rome).
1672.

Pietro Tempesta (c. 1637-1701):
Drawing-room, Palazzo Colonna, Rome.
1668.

many reminders of antiquity, and their presence in the room is as incongruous as would be that of an archaeological find. In the past, apart from a few chairs, a single object formed the centre of interest of this room space: an *occhialone* or spy-glass, which afforded the visitor an evasion towards even more distant spaces, out to the horizon of the Roman Campagna. At the height of the Baroque period, the Romantic taste for nature and ruins was already alive.

For the trompe-l'œil painter, nothing is too remote, nothing is impossible. By this means, one of the drawing-rooms in the Palazzo Colonna in Rome opens on to the sea. Dark and storm-tossed on one side, glowing in the sun and calm as a mirror on the other, the sea surrounds this room as if it were an island, a haven of peace. Painted by Modanino, some fleshy and colourful Atlases support the simulated vaults and arcades. [21] Their improbable, Manneristic presence emphasizes, by contrast, the cosmic dimension of Pietro Tempesta's continuous landscape. [22] In the Palazzo Colonna, the opening up of the barrier wall permits the artist, and spectator, to reach beyond land and sea into the remoteness of infinity.

Charles Louis Clérisseau (1722-1820):
Monastery of Trinità dei Monti, Rome.
1766.

From the monastic seclusion of their cell in the monastery of Trinità dei Monti in Rome, Friars Le Sueur and Jacquier were able, thanks to Clérisseau's fresco, to escape into the world of antiquity which must have haunted their imagination, being ever present in the books they read. This French painter working in Rome, a pupil of Natoire, unified the ceiling and walls, thereby transforming the narrow cell space into the picturesque ruin of a pagan temple.[23] The cell of the two monks became a place of pilgrimage for Roman art-lovers and intellectuals. Much admired by the Adam brothers, Winckelmann and Mengs, this decoration was one of the first works to embody that "mania for the antique" (in Diderot's words) which characterized the Neoclassicism soon to come. A contemporary gives a vivid description of it: "It was like walking into the cell of a temple enriched with ancient fragments which had survived the ravages of time. The vault and some stretches of dilapidated walls, supported by ill-joined timberwork, let the sky through and seemed to give passage to rays of sunlight. These effects rendered with skill and accuracy produce a complete illusion. To enhance it more pointedly still, all the furniture shared the same character. The bed was a basin..., the fireplace a collection of miscellaneous fragments, the desk an ancient disfigured sarcophagus... Even the dog faithfully watching over this furniture of a new kind was kennelled in a shattered vase."[24]

Ambiguous, like the optical and occult sciences cultivated by the Friars Minim of Trinità dei Monti, this space is at the same time a humble thebaid of hermits and a decoration for a classical comedy. Here once again, the trompe-l'œil remains faithful to its ludic role.[25]

It is not always necessary to do away with the wall in order to make evasion possible. A simulated window in a dark cool space may also introduce light and give a glimpse of the wonders of a non-existent garden.

If the window always remains shut, one can escape through the dark and mysterious chink of the secret door and enter the "beyond" of the wall, with the hope of finding there the radiant and transparent world of fanciful palaces.

Palazzo del Quirinale, Rome.
18th century.

Andrea Sighizzi (died 1684):
Palazzo Reale, Genoa.
17th century.

With the same facility, trompe-l'œil may rule out any evasion. Then the doors which it creates are forever shut and the sham stage curtain waits to be lifted. There ends the play.

Signatures

After the fall of the curtain, the players take their bow and acknowledge the applause. The painters of simulated architecture cannot sign their works: to do so would be a betrayal of the trompe-l'œil. So to make their appearance, they introduce their self-portrait and take their place in the illusionist decor.

In the Villa Falconieri at Frascati, the painter Pier Leone Ghezzi is seated on the edge of the simulated balustrade which separates the drawing-room from the fine terrace and garden. Behind the simulated window, half open, is a Capuchin monk, while the painter in court dress can be seen drawing. He gazes straight at the spectator. Does he see the spectator or is it his own reflection that he is looking at in a non-existent mirror? The ambiguity of the self-portrait and that of the trompe-l'œil here intersect, like questioning glances. The artist's gaze holds us fast and obliges us to decipher the inscription on the base: "Ghezzius hic faciem gestus se pinxit et artem sed magnum ingenium pingere non potuit." The artist painted his own features and showed his art, but the great qualities of the inner man he could not render.

Antonio Galli Bibiena and his assistants had no hesitation about giving themselves what they considered to be their due.[26] Defying time and the chances of success, they set up their busts while they were still alive in the simulated niches, where in time to come they would adorn the drawing-room of their

△ Josef Lederer (mid-18th century):
Self-Portrait with Cup of Coffee.
Hall of Masks, Castle of Česky-Krumlov,
Czechoslovakia.
1748.

◁ Pier Leone Ghezzi (1674-1755):
Parlour (Stanza delle Conversazioni),
Villa Falconieri, Frascati (Rome).
1727.

Verona patrons. Such was the sublime self-assurance of these artists at the height of their fame.

In the Castle of Česky-Krumlov (Bohemia), the painted architecture creates a dreamworld repeated a hundredfold by the mirror reflections. Transformed into a playhouse, the walls of the room open on to boxes and galleries which, oddly enough, extend into gardens. Figures from the *commedia dell'arte* mingle with the public, and Prince Schwarzenberg himself is attending the performance.[27] Nobles and peasants rub shoulders. Turning his back on this scene which he glances at with wandering eyes, the painter Josef

Lederer has finished his work and is sipping coffee. His name is inscribed like an ornament on the coffee pot. By thus bringing himself forward and apart, the artist no longer participates in the masquerade. As its aloof creator, he dominates it.

Another painter, in North Italy, signs his work with modesty and humour: Carlo Carlone. His name is inscribed in tiny letters on the collar of the *carlin* (pug-dog) proudly walking in front of its masters on the steps of this imaginary palace. Witty and discreet, the written message accompanies and concludes the trompe-l'œil.

△ Antonio Galli Bibiena (1700-1774)
and collaborators:
Drawing-room, Casa Ferrari-Cartolari, Verona:
Artist portraits.
1765.

◁ Carlo Carlone (1686-1775):
Detail of the drawing-room,
villa near Brescia, North Italy.
1745.

5
Space
Reconsidered

Giovan Battista Piranesi (1720-1778):
Wall decoration, English Coffee House, Rome.
Print from his *Diverse maniere*, 1769.

◁ Palazzo del Quirinale, Rome:
Hall of the Piedmontese Tapestries.
Late 19th century.

Both the strict-mindedness of Neoclassicism and the purely decorative vocation of *Barocchetto* or Rococo drained trompe-l'œil of its substance and made it pointless. Later on, the coming of the industrial age marked its decline. The taste for an elegant and witty subterfuge which took its place in experienced reality was replaced by a picturesque and eclectic ostentation. Quality decoration came to draw on essentially different sources. It found its beauty in the visual richness of coloured ceramics or in the linear finesse of stucco or wrought metal. Even so, the search for an illusion of reality did not cease to exist. It is to be found elsewhere, often outside the inhabited space. Arising in reaction against the heavy eclecticism of the nineteenth century, modern architecture created an objective space requiring a bare wall, capable of catching light and generating volumes. Such a wall could tolerate no decoration. The presence here of an architectural trompe-l'œil would have had no sense. The increasing banalization of the architecture of the 1930s, by then functional first and foremost, led to a renewed, refelt need for an imaginary space breaking the monotony of the same standard units repeated *ad infinitum*. Today trompe-l'œil has been reborn. Often nostalgic for the past, it also raises once again the fundamental issue of the pictorial representation of a third dimension.

Eclecticism and dissolution

When the surroundings of a lived-in space were changed by a painted decoration, no attempt was necessarily made to retain the plausibility of the architectural setting which opened the door of the imaginary. What was aimed at was the creation of unfamiliar surroundings, unfamiliar both in time and space. So it is that Piranesi, a precursor but one fully aware of the taste of his day, did not hesitate to create "Egyptian" settings long before Napoleon's expeditions made them popular. He thus had the extravagant idea of

Pietro Baldancoli (1834-1901):
Drawing-room, Palazzo Serristori, Florence.
1896-1897.

painting the walls of the English Coffee House in the Piazza di Spagna in Rome with improbable architectures opening on to "pyramids and sepulchres in the desert" and on to "the fertile plain of the Nile."[1] Adorned with an incredible profusion of scarabs, sphinxes and gods, also with grasshoppers and crocodiles, these decorations embody the imaginings of an artist enamoured of archaeology. The fact is that Piranesi entertained theories of his own connecting the civilization of Egypt with that of the Etruscans — i.e. with Rome.

Considered too gloomy for the needs of a place where English tourists foregathered, this wall painting in a Roman café was soon effaced, but the taste for such pastiches was only at its beginnings.

Once it had reached the point where the work of the *quadraturisti* merged with that of the stucco-workers, goldsmiths, bronzesmiths, iron-workers and stone-carvers, the architectural trompe-l'œil often lost all meaning and departed from its figural character. Whether they were real or simulated, the result, in rooms meant for show, was the perfect correspondence of wall and ceiling ornaments, of wrought-iron balustrades and stuccoes, of the volutes, shellwork, corkscrews and festoons of the panelling.

Carrying this dissolution through to the end, the painted decoration of the late nineteenth century in the Hall of Piedmontese Tapestries in the Quirinal palace in Rome takes over the themes and handling of the Orientalizing embroideries adorning the partition walls. It forms an arabesque of aerial trellis-work supporting weightless vases, against a background which seems like an extension of the precious and silky fabrics covering the walls. Butterflies and soap bubbles emphasize the transient unreality of this painting which is no longer a trompe-l'œil of architecture but one of tapestry.

The main drawing-room of the Palazzo Serristori in Florence was destroyed by fire in 1866, and Umberto Serristori had it rebuilt and redecorated in 1897. On the wall, for posterity, the painter Pietro Baldancoli recorded the fact that he reproduced the old wall paintings and that he "invented" and "designed" the frieze and the vault. But his work does not amount to the restoration of a simulated architecture, such as had been done in Florence in the past. Anaemic and pale, it remains an astonishing decoration done "in the manner'' of the style of a bygone day. Lifeless and frigid, it is in the image of the factitious, washed-out sky which it discloses. The ''Baroque'' which the painter has set out to evoke is remote indeed.

It was perhaps a ''restoration,'' once again, that the church council of Chambéry, in Savoy, thought it was ordering for the local cathedral. The contract shows that, for this severe Franciscan church erected in the fifteenth and sixteenth century, the councillors specifically commissioned from the painter Casimir Vicario a trompe-l'œil decoration in a Flamboyant Gothic style whose excesses have a curiously English flavour. ''The church council has adopted the style of Gothic painting as being the one most in harmony with the edifice. [The painter] shall provide a curvilinear pediment... its mouldings adorned with leafage... in keeping with the taste of the day,'' stipulates the contract.[2] Vicario himself, however, does not seem to have been whole-hearted about this troubadour-Gothic decoration. For in replying in the local paper, the *Courrier des Alpes*, to the sharp criticism of a reader who found the church ''rather too bare and heavy... overloaded on all its walls with frescoes in bad taste,'' Vicario explained that the architect in charge of restoration, ''talented in architecture to a rare degree but too little versed in the Gothic style, had engaged the artist... to avoid straight lines, one of the characteristic features of *Arab-German* architecture, improperly known as *Gothic*: one may therefore understand why the eye gets weary following up an endless variety of curves instead of coming to rest on straight lines.'' Vicario found an excuse for the orgy of lierne-ribs and secondary ribs whose eddies and whirls bewilder the eye: according to him, ''these originalities are quite permissible, in view of the fact that the construction of the metropolitan church goes back to the period of *decadence.*''[3] What a tissue of misunderstandings behind this dazzling and luminous decoration! The painter really had no need to excuse himself for a work so very much in the fashion of the day. The church council could not have chosen a decoration more in keeping with what was then considered, in Paris and elsewhere, as the quintessence of good taste, that of the Gothic Revival.

So little by little the spirit and forthrightness of architectural trompe-l'œil disappeared, both in secular room spaces and in churches. The pastiches of anti-

Casimir Vicario (early 19th century):
Chambéry Cathedral (Savoy).
1833.

quity, of Renaissance art and Gothic, together with the *turqueries* and *chinoiseries*, succeeded in agreeably flattering the eye and imagination; but they did not, they could not, by their very eclecticism, set up for being a substitute for reality. And no one was taken in, or even pretended to be.

Another illusion

In the nineteenth century, the urban home interior no longer lent itself in the same way to the play of illusionism. Its flower designs and its sumptuous draperies taken over by painted panels had no more than the symbolic role of a quotation. The metamorphosis which they produced in the room space, already overloaded with furniture and ornaments, was purely aesthetic and decorative. Wallpaper, soon to be dispensed by the yard, was never able, even for a moment, to transform a living-room into a bucolic garden.[4] Even less was it able to simulate the "Flamboyant Gothic-style château" which moreover had never existed outside the imagination of fashionable novelists. On the other hand, "thanks to machine printing, it was possible to produce very cheap wallpapers and bring to the home interior a luxury and comfort accessible now to all classes of society."[5]

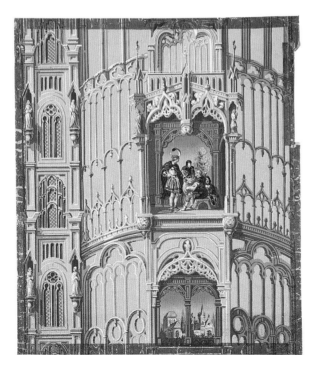

Wallpaper.
1835-1840.

However far from creating illusion, wallpaper certainly remained a social reality.

Stained-glass windows, having become the ornament of middleclass homes, also contributed to create this allusion to unfamiliar surroundings. By filtering the city light into shimmering colours, they brought into late nineteenth century homes a view over exotic gardens or marvellous palaces.[6] Thus isolated by "image-screens" from the world around it, the home turned in upon itself and gained in intimacy.

In order to reach places where the game of illusion was really accepted and could be experienced as a truth, the Parisian spectator had to leave his apartment and go some distance from the centre of the city. At the end of his jaunt, along the tree-planted boulevards, he came to the Panorama Rotunda. Here, in this rotunda, he was confronted with the fascinating invention of the Edinburgh artist, Robert Barker, designed to satisfy the quest for another reality than that of everyday life.[7] But to reach it he had to go through a dark labyrinth of passages and stairs which made him lose all sense of space and distance. In this way he forgot that he was in a round building, massive as a watchtower, in the fortress of the collective imagination. Suddenly space opened out and the spectator found himself on a circular platform, lighted from above. His eye then took in the continuous view of a landscape painted on the distant horizon.[8] Having lost the sense of reality, with no material frame of reference to guide him, he felt himself engulfed in infinite space. Each spectator had the impression of being the centre of this artificial world which he dominated from his high point of observation. While belonging to it, he was isolated from it, standing in apparent solitude and perfect security. By means of this panorama mounted on a cylindrical surface, he could visit distant cities and witness battles and sea fights.[9] Standing on the hazy borderline separating the true from the sham, he himself played an ambiguous part somewhere between a spectator and an actor.

Before the canvases of the Dioramas invented by Daguerre, canvases ingeniously painted on both sides and illuminated by reflection as well as by trans-

Robert Mitchell (active 1782-1801):
Section of his Rotunda in Leicester Square,
London, with Robert Barker's Panorama paintings.
1801.

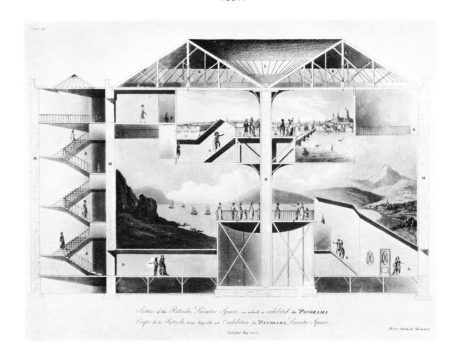

parency, the spectator here played a well-defined part. Detached from reality by an approach through dark passages, he was seated on a turning platform where, quite passive, he was carried from one huge picture to another. The views he gazed at served as framework for no particular action. They were presented, vividly presented, for their own sake. In them, day gave place to night, storms blew up, rivers overflowed, all to a musical accompaniment. The painted panels of Daguerre's Dioramas, which for half a century attracted crowds in Paris and other cities, have all been destroyed by fires.[10] The only remaining relics of them are a few prints and paintings made by the artist himself. Their almost tactile realism accounts for the illusion of perfect "mimesis" which these showings seem to have created for enthusiastic audiences in the nineteenth century.[11]

Thus the desire to enjoy the outside world while remaining indoors, to seek out distant horizons without bothering to move, was satisfied by devices constructed for this purpose, in the taste of the period. Museums, galleries, panoramas and dioramas provided a host of people with the illusions of reality.

Jacques Daguerre (1787-1851):
Ruins of Holyrood Chapel, Edinburgh.
Oil painting after his Diorama.
1824.

93

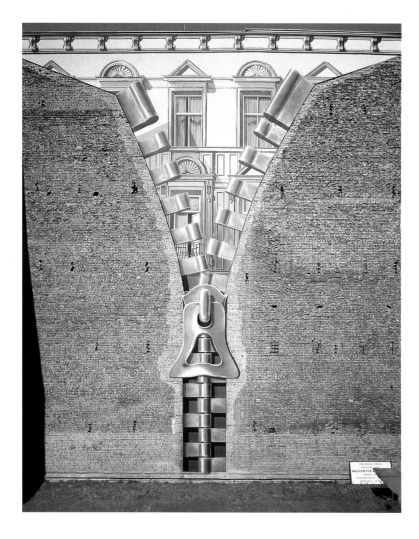

Gert Neuhaus (1939):
Zipper, painted wall in Berlin.
1979.

In the nineteenth century, the taste for simulated appearances was revived by the desire to make "being" and "seeming" coincide. The subterfuge was a searching one, going beyond a mere modification of the surface by overpainting it. The whole design of new buildings contributed to transform factories and stations into churches, and town houses into castles.[14] Façade decoration became three-dimensional; columns and mouldings reappeared and metal wrought in lacework went to form the framework. So it was that, when later the taste for nature and craftwork metamorphosed façades into walls with floral designs, it was ceramic tiles and mosaics, not painting, which brought back the element of colour to the house-fronts of the city.

Kenn White:
Painted façade, London.
About 1979.

Contestation

Throughout history, façades have been painted. Non-figurative polychrome images in antiquity, they assumed in the Middle Ages the aspect of the architectural trompe-l'œil. Their obvious purpose was to embellish the building by conferring on it something of the splendour and richness which it could achieve in no other way. It was also a rapid and effective means of overlaying antiquated buildings with an outward aspect of symmetry and harmony. Acting as the surface of contact between the palace and the villa, the façade decoration often played a didactic and political role. With the erosion of individual power and of the cult of personality, they became a means of visually unifying a neighbourhood, as part of a larger concern to beautify the city.[12] Weather, passing time and changing mentalities have made for the disappearance of most of the older painted façades. If many painted windows have survived in Italy, it is only thanks to the fiscal laws, while in the Germanic lands a love of the picturesque and a proud sense of inheritance have maintained down to today the tradition of the "fine" façade.[13] Elsewhere it was the natural colour of the building materials that usually replaced the colours provided by painting.

The pressure of social conditions, the evolution of techniques and materials, the new aesthetics in revolt against the traditional figural art, above all the reaction against the stifling eclecticism of the nineteenth century, contributed to the creation of what we call "modern architecture." In the event, our century has witnessed a profound change in the very definition of the architectural space. Having become free, volume has been substituted for mass, mobility for static rigidity, transparency for decorative suffocation. In this objective space the outer wall could tolerate no mystification. It had to remain bare and proclaim its function. The trompe-l'œil façade was obviously banished from the glassed-in skyscraper. Its specular surfaces, rendered mobile by the gleaming reflections of sky and clouds, could not be decorated.

The introduction of lighter techniques, of prefabricated parts and synthetic materials, in conjunction with modern economic and social conditions, had the effect (on the plea of safeguarding its functional and rational design) of denaturing the purity of the new architecture. Vulgarized, commercialized and repeated *ad nauseam*, these buildings became "monotonous, expressionless and one-dimensional."[15] War and its blind ravages, alterations and the chaotic spread of the urban space, revealed only too plainly the lack of any regulating plan and the difficulty of interconnection. Thus the townscape became punctuated with the bare walls, peeling gables and desolate backyards of outlandish buildings. These remnants of abandoned or broken-down constructions now came to serve as the picture surface of a new kind of painting. This surface was often seized on for aggressive publicity or transformed into a political manifesto by an ephemeral, anonymous, sometimes clandestine painting. When contemporary artists took possession of the wall, they made it the place of their intervention in the aspect and structure of the city. They made themselves the spokesmen of the people living in the neighbourhood, of the unknown passerby, and in their name voiced the desire for change. If it was to be integrated into the surrounding architecture (even while standing apart from it), the wall painting also had to have the consensus of the local authorities and that in some cases of a sponsor. The conjunction was complex and difficult to achieve.[16] It was not a question, as in the past, of ennobling a façade, but rather of abolishing or transforming a barrier that jarred.

Hence the zipper painted by Gert Neuhaus: in place of the bare gabled wall, it opens by an act of magic and brings forth a new architecture whose tranquil, luminous symmetry recalls an imaginary past. On a wall in Berlin, this message has the potency of a symbol.[17] In London, Kenn White brightens with a blue patch the monotonous surface of a row of suburban houses.

The solution is pleasant, but the implication is brutal, for in order to make a patch of blue sky appear, it is necessary first of all to demolish the decaying architecture of the past.

"The city has an image, it is full of simulations and façades, it is a big apartment which tells the story of the people who have lived in that place."[18] It was as an artist in love with the city and its past that Fabio Rieti painted a bare wall in the port of Marseilles: on it he catches, as in a mirror, the imposing masses of the fort of Saint-Jean and the Sainte-Marie lighthouse, while a schooner projects its majestic silhouette in the foreground. The presence of the boat asserts the desire to preserve the unity of the old port, and protect it against any intrusion from outside.

Richard Haas (1936):
Painted wall, Boston Architectural Center.
1975-1977.

The Boston Architectural Center rises over the roofs of one of the older sections of the city, and skyscrapers act as a distant backdrop to it. If the front and sides of the building remain in the discreet shadow cast by the projections of the attic, the rear wall, on the other hand, visible from a distance, catches all the light on its smooth and aggressive surface. It is on this rear wall that Richard Haas and his team of sign painters depicted a memorial of past architecture, and there Haas implicitly asserted his options for an architecture of the future. Obviously based on Beaux-Arts drawings and Prix de Rome designs of the nineteenth century, and on the visions of Boullée and Ledoux, this cross-section cutaway view is a justifiable choice in the context of the Architectural Center which it adorns. The unobtrusive presence of a few human figures introduces that provocative ambiguity which trompe-l'œil painting has always permitted. They are, as Haas has written, "an additional element in the mural, allowing the viewer to bring his own fantasies and illusions to the piece."[19] A trompe-l'œil of reality? By no means. What we have rather is an oversized semblance of the fine working drawing, the design for an architecture which, as the artist expressly wished, has its roots in the past.

Nostalgias

Born of the reaction against the hidebound rigidity of nineteenth century residential dwellings, "modern architecture" has defined a new interior space. Whether concentrated (Le Corbusier) or fluid (Mies van der Rohe), this space aims at making indistinct, undiscernible, the limits between interior and exterior. The introduction of horizontal "panoramic" windows and privileged points of view tends to bring the spectacular perspectives of the surrounding world into the middleclass interior and so makes any pictorial fiction uncalled-for.[20] Bearing structures, moreover, are reduced to a minimum, and the space can be divided up by thin, movable partitions whose sculptural shape and position constitute the sole ornament. In this rational space, the wall has to be bare and light-attracting: it is self-sufficing and cannot be decorated. An architectural trompe-l'œil would have been unthinkable in the context of Neo-Plasticism, with its two-dimensional world of monochrome planes and surfaces.

The trend of this so-called "modern" architecture towards uniformity and denaturing, together with the slow asphyxia of its "functional" and "rational" conception of space, have led today to the reappearance of architectural trompe-l'œil. Its return probably answers to the need to reintroduce into architecture a pictorial and plastic element; but it also voices a protest, a contestation, a rejection. As so often in the past, trompe-l'œil proceeds to abolish existing structures, thereby enabling the eye to escape into a world which has now assumed the likeness of a dream. Steeped in the experience of Surrealism, it challenges reality while focusing on emphatic details of it. Paul Delvaux offers a telling example: in a Brussels house he painted a fresco in which the interior mingles with the exterior and antiquity with the contemporary world, in an impossible palace architecture. Dali, on the other hand, turns back to the Renaissance and,

following Mantegna's example, opens up the vault, where the shade of the eternal Gala is made to appear, and where he places a balustrade over which hangs a "limp watch."[21]

The return to an artistic past has become today like a leitmotiv. The landscapes evoked are rarely in the likeness of the city outside, but suggestive rather of distant countries where the sun is always shining. Thus Venice, Florence, Rome, Geneva and perhaps Jerusalem are brought together in a dream to make up the decoration imagined by the Vaisseau group in Geneva. Here one discovers ironic but relevant quotations, together with ceilings "in the manner of Carlone" and floating curtains "in the manner of Daret."

In this glittering kaleidoscope which lights up the blind stair-well of an escalator, one detects the amused but nostalgic gaze of today's generation, looking back at the works of yesterday.

Vaisseau Group
with the collaboration of Emmanuelle Ambrosetti:
Wall decoration, Geneva.
1983.

Davide Boriani (1936):
Architecture of the past, Pavia.
1975.

up to the imaginary attic. In this way it promises access to non-existent spaces which would impart to this interior the unique and festive aspect to which it aspires.

Nostalgic, ironic, picturesque or bantering, the trompe-l'œil of today also runs the risk, sometimes, of becoming a decorative surface element of which one may soon get tired, as one does of a faded curtain. Yet, over and above anecdote, it conveys a desire to live in a different environment where dream and fantasy take over from the useful and uniform.

Baudouin de Renty (1957)
and
Philippe de Lanouvelle (1957):
Belle Epoque staircase, Paris.
1984.

Elegant and monochrome, the staircase painted by Davide Boriani in a house at Pavia, in North Italy, is like the fleeting apparition of a *scala maestra* in the palaces of yesterday. Turning upon itself and disappearing upwards, it cannot lead anywhere. It seems to be haunted by Piranesi and Bibiena. Yet the artist seeks out his purity of line further back in the past, in the vestiges of a Baroque trompe-l'œil standing in the entrance courtyard. A mixture of styles, a refining of intentions, an evocation of the past by way of trompe-l'œil, have found in this old house in the historic centre of Pavia a *raison d'être* with deep-lying roots.

The Belle Epoque staircase by Baudouin de Renty and Philippe de Lanouvelle masks the embarrassing presence of an armoured door. It lights up a blind entrance, and to a modern apartment on one level it gives the sweep of a third dimension which it lacked. Attached to reality, the staircase takes over the white frames of the other doors and prolongs the red carpet

Perspectives

Departing from the strict definition of trompe-l'œil, present-day artists raise with acuity the fundamental problem of represented space and its relation to reality. They courageously question the concepts in terms of which the picture surface may become the projection plane of created space by means of the perspective illusion. By doing so, they challenge the fundamental endeavour of illusionist painting to extend real space by fictive space.

Lessing (quoted by Panofsky) describes perspective as the "science of representing several objects together with the part of space in which they stand, so that the notion of the picture as material support is driven out by the notion of a transparent plane which, as we believe, our gaze traverses in order to plunge into an imaginary outer space containing all these objects in apparent sequence, an unbounded space merely cut off by the edges of the picture."[22]

As if to emphasize the postulates implied by spatial representation in accordance with the rules of perspective, Paolini reverses all the roles. In his *De Pictura* he displays a series of nine panels which delimit the visual field. In the centre, an overturned panel shows the dark, opaque canvas covering the stretcher. It has a dual purpose. By contrast, the white panels surrounding it become transparent and take the place of the Albertian "window" over which should be projected the image of the space beyond the wall. Further, the "overturned picture" repudiates its own function as the support of an image in real space and implies that it regains that function in the imaginary space where it becomes visible only for the phantom spectator who inhabits it. "I always use such figures as are capable of becoming images, both for the spectator and for myself... The image is something which does not exist in itself... which comes from afar and also goes far," writes Paolini.[23]

By setting out in unfathomable depth a representation of space which is at the same time object and image, the painter cancels out the signification of perspective and that of the single vanishing point.[24] So it is that, at our option, real space or imaginary space is, in a perfect equivalence, the specular reflection of the other.

Giulio Paolini (1940):
De Pictura.
1979.

Felice Varini (1952):
View: Young Sculpture, Port of Austerlitz, Paris.
May 1985.

The linear pattern of the surfaces is developed on walls which delimit in depth a receding sequence of complex volumes. Felice Varini thus achieves "in given spaces certain pictorial interventions deriving directly from the information which space gives him."[25]

The fictive volumes thus created by the artist can only be coherently apprehended from a particular spot. The viewpoint of *perspettiva legittima* imposed on the spectator here assumes its extreme form, that of a point without dimensions. By an extrapolation of perspective methods carried to their limits, Varini situates his work, like an anamorphosis, at the opposite pole from trompe-l'œil. He thereby critically defines the domain of its possible existence.

The cube and the frustum of a pyramid, both aggressive by their very size, float in the undefined space between our own and the one beyond the wall. The axonometric projection in bird's-eye view that Sol LeWitt has chosen preserves the form and dimensions of the elevation and shortens the recessions. The vanishing lines will never meet, and they may extend in front of the wall just as well as behind it. The eye thus becomes completely free to contemplate the image which, in the words of Malevich, "breaks with the earth."[26] Vision being liberated, the eye ceases to be held in thrall and perspective no longer means constraint. The trompe-l'œil has become abstract and as such dissolves in the infinite.

Sol LeWitt (1928):
Forms Derived from a Cube.
1982.

Philippe Granvelle (1954):
Visions.
1980.

Finale

At the end of the road, one may ask whether the architectural trompe-l'œil of tomorrow must necessarily stand in opposition to its support, hollowing out what was meant to be full and opening up what was meant to be closed. By multiplying the planes of reference and specular surface reflections, by means of simulated materials and false scales, the trompe-l'œil in untrammelled freedom might be able to search out new spaces. As the imaginary image of a dream reality, as the flight of the eye towards distant horizons, it might be able to assume a place of its own in the eventual creation of an organic architecture set free from hidebound formulas and designs—an architecture whose dynamics would be able to make play with an ambiguous space. Perhaps, then, the renaissance of a certain Baroque...

Notes and References

Prelude (page 6)

1   These phrases appeared as the superscription to an article by Jean Baudrillard on "The Precession of Simulacra" in *Traverses*, 10, Paris, February 1978, page 3. There they were given as coming from *Ecclesiastes*. By thus attributing what in fact was his own, the author of the article achieved an exemplary simulacrum, for the "true" and the "false" have remained indistinguishable to this day. Our thanks are due to Jean Baudrillard for confessing to us that he wrote the phrases himself, and allowing us to reattribute them here.

Chapter 1 (page 9)

1   Painted architecture at Pompeii is discussed here without taking any account of the so-called four styles defined by August Mau at the end of the 19th century.
    See I. Lavin, "The Ceiling Frescoes in Trier and Illusionism in Constantinian Painting," *Dumbarton Oaks Papers*, 21, Washington, 1967, p. 99.
    L. Curtius, *Die Wandmalerei Pompejis*, Leipzig, 1929.
    A. Maiuri, *Roman Painting*, Geneva - New York, 1953.

2   For the interpretation of Vitruvius' text, see E. Panofsky, "Die Perspektive als symbolische Form," *Vorträge der Bibliothek Warburg*, 1924-1925, p. 258 ff.

3   See E. Börsch-Supan, *Garten-, Landschafts- und Paradiesmotive im Innenraum*, Berlin, 1967, p. 64.

4   Nero's Golden House is described by Suetonius in *The Lives of the Caesars*, Loeb, London and Cambridge, Mass., 1914.

5   See S. Giedion, *Architecture and the Phenomena of Transition*, Cambridge, Mass., 1971, p. 160.

6   These Assisi frescoes are now attributed to a "Gothic workshop" of about 1270, preceding Cimabue in the church.
    See H. Belting, *Die Oberkirche von San Francesco in Assisi*, Berlin, 1977.

7   Inscription in the upper part of the fresco.
    See A. Jaques, "La fresque funéraire de l'église Saint-Maurice," *Annesci*, 1956, p. 105.
    According to C. Gardet, *De la peinture du Moyen Age en Savoie*, I, Annecy, 1965, p. 127, the Saint-Maurice fresco stands in the tradition of the schools of Conrad Witz and Giacomo Jacquerio.

8   The tomb of Philip the Bold is now in the Musée des Beaux-Arts, Dijon.

9   W. Paesseler, "Der Rückgriff der römischen Spätdugentomalerei auf die christliche Spätantike," *Beiträge zur Kunst des Mittelalters*, Berlin, 1950, p. 157.
    H. Toubert, "Le renouveau paléochrétien à Rome au début du XIIe siècle," *Cahiers archéologiques*, 1970, 20, p. 99.

10 See K. Stamm, *Probleme des Bildes und der Dekoration in mittelitalienischen Freskenzyklen der Zeit um 1300 bis in die Mitte des Quattrocento*, dissertation, Bonn, 1974, p. 18.

11 The fresco cycle of the life of St Francis is attributed to painters working in Giotto's entourage.
    See H. Belting, *Die Oberkirche von San Francesco in Assisi*, Berlin, 1977.

12 G.L. Mellini, *Altichiero e Jacopo Avanzo*, Milan, 1965.

13 When the loggia is seen from in front, the perspective effect conceals the pilaster behind the pillar. When the panels are seen from an angle, the structure of the simulated architecture can be better understood. Unfortunately these panels are in poor condition. The fresco is documented as being the work of Giovanni del Sega (1506).
    See A. Garuti, "Decorazioni esterne a Carpi e nel suo territorio. Testimonianze dal XV all'inizio del XX secolo," *Facciate dipinte, conservazione e restauro, Atti del convegno di studi*, Genoa, 15-17 April 1982, p. 50.

14 L. Berti, *Il museo di Palazzo Davanzati a Firenze*, Milan, 1972.
    E. Borsook, *The Mural Painters of Tuscany from Cimabue to Andrea del Sarto*, Oxford, 1980, p. 55.

15 *La Chastelaine de Vergi*, French poem of the 13th century, edited by G. Raynaud, Paris, 1979.

Notes and References

The choice of theme may have been influenced by the similarity between ''Castelana,'' the bride's name, and the ''Chastelaine'' (i.e. châtelaine) of the poem.

16 L.B. Alberti, *L'architettura*, book IX, chapter IV, Milan, 1966, p. 805.

17 N. Rasmò, *Castelroncolo*, Bolzano, 1967, 3rd edition, 1975.
N. Rasmò, *Affreschi medioevali atesini*, Milan, 1971.

18 J. Weingartner, *Die Kunstdenkmale des Etschlandes*, Vienna, 1926, p. 182, quoted in A. Morassi, *Storia della pittura nella Venezia Tridentina*, Rome, 1923, p. 302.

19 J. Marcuse, *Bäder und Badewesen*, Stuttgart, 1903, p. 67.
L. Wright, *Clean and Decent: The Fascinating History of the Bathroom and the Water Closet*, London, 1984, p. 58.

20 Vitruvius, *Les dix livres d'architecture*, French translation by Claude Perrault, 1673, revised by André Dalmas, Paris, 1979, p. 173. English translation, *On Architecture*, Loeb, London and Cambridge, Mass., 1931-1934.

21 N. Rasmò, *Il Castello del Buonconsiglio a Trento*, Cassa di Risparmio di Torino.

22 On the months, see O. Pächt, ''Early Italian Nature Studies and the Early Calendar Landscapes,'' *Journal of the Warburg and Courtauld Institute*, XIII, 1950, p. 13.

23 In his life of Augustus, Suetonius refers to the emperor's *studiolo*: ''Erat illi locus in edito singularis... quid secreto aut sine interpellatione agere proposuisset.''
A reconstruction of Augustus's *studiolo*, made from small fragments found on the Palatine, was recently exhibited. It was a small cubic room, four metres square and four metres high, frescoed with simulated architectures opening on landscapes. See G. Musatti and R. Motta, *Gli affreschi della Casa di Augusto sul Palatino*, exhibition *Restauri al Palazzo Altemps*, Rome, June 1985.
On the iconography and history of the *studiolo*, see W. Liebenwein, *Studiolo – Die Entstehung eines Raumtyps und seine Entwicklung bis 1600*, Berlin, 1977, and F. Deuchler, ''Maximilian I. und die Kaiserviten Suetons,'' *Von Angesicht zu Angesicht: Michael Stettler zum 70. Geburtstag: Porträtstudien*, Berne, 1983, p. 135.

24 Proverbs viii.3 and ix.14.

25 For the references to Pliny the Younger, Pliny the Elder and Petrarch, see W. Liebenwein, *Studiolo – Die Entstehung eines Raumtyps...*, Berlin, 1977.

26 The *studiolo* of the Medici (c. 1464) had a ceiling adorned with twelve majolica tondi by Luca della Robbia, representing the labours of the months, the phases of the day and night, and the signs of the zodiac.
See J. Pope Hennessy, *Catalogue of Italian Sculptures in the Victoria and Albert Museum*, I, 1964, p. 104, and P. Bresciani, *Figurazioni dei mesi nell'arte medioevale italiana*, Verona, 1968.
The Torre Aquila fresco is known to have been restored from 1534 on, chiefly in the upper part with the sky. So it is not unreasonable to suppose that around the sun, as in della Robbia's tondi, the phases of the day and night may have been indicated.
See A. Morassi, ''Come il Fogolino restaurò gli affreschi di Torre Aquila a Trento,'' *Bollettino d'Arte*, February 1929, p. 337.

27 This fresco in the Palazzo della Signoria, now much faded, is attributed to Stradanus.

28 As suggested by W. Liebenwein, *Studiolo – Die Entstehung eines Raumtyps...*, Berlin, 1977.

Chapter 2 (page 27)

1 E. Panofsky, ''Die Perspektive als symbolische Form,'' *Vorträge der Bibliothek Warburg*, 1924-1925.

2 S. Czymmek, *Die architektur-illusionistische Deckenmalerei in Italien und Deutschland von den Anfängen bis in die Zeit um 1700*, dissertation, Mainz, 1978, p. 19.

3 Francesco di Giorgio Martini quoted in Czymmek, op. cit., p. 35, note 22. Marc Antonio Altieri, *Le Nuptiali*, quoted in Czymmek, p. 21, note 28.

4 M. Kraitrova, ''Das Haus von Andrea Mantegna in Mantua und von Piero della Francesca in Sansepolcro,'' *Künstler-Häuser von der Renaissance bis zur Gegenwart*, Munich, 1985, pp. 51-56.

5 F. Würtenberger, ''Die manieristische Deckenmalerei in Mittelitalien,'' *Römisches Jahrbuch für Kunstgeschichte*, 4, Vienna, 1940, p. 109.
I. Mussa, ''L'architettura illusionistica nelle decorazioni romane,'' *Capitolium*, 8/9, 1969, pp. 41-88.
M.C. Gloton, *Trompe-l'œil et décor plafonnant dans les églises romaines de l'âge baroque*, Rome, 1965, pp. 140-146.

6 E. Börsch-Supan, *Garten-, Landschafts- und Paradiesmotive im Innenraum*, Berlin, 1967, pp. 244-260.

7 The conception of the Vatican Loggie is generally attributed to Raphael. The painted architecture is attributed to Peruzzi by K. Lanckoronska, ''Zu Raphaels Loggien,'' *Jahrbuch der kunsthistorischen Sammlungen in Wien*, N.F. IX, 1935, p. 111.

8 See Chapter 1, page 9 (Modification).

9 Ingrid Sjöström, *Quadratura: Studies in Italian Ceiling Painting*, Stockholm, 1978, p. 49.

10 T. Poensgen, *Die Deckenmalerei in italienischen Kirchen*, Berlin, 1969, p. 76.
I Campi e la cultura artistica cremonese del Cinquecento, exhibition catalogue, Cremona, 1985.

11 E. Gavazza, *La grande decorazione a Genova*, Genoa, 1974, pp. 114 and 214.

12 The rivalry and ill-temper of Ansaldo and Benso were such that they actually came to blows. See R. Soprani and C.G. Ratti, *Vite de' pittori, scultori ed architetti genovesi*, Bologna, 1969, p. 205.

13 E. Gavazza, *La grande decorazione a Genova*, Genoa, 1974, p. 264.

14 C.L. Frommel, *Die Farnesina und Peruzzis architektonisches Frühwerk*, Berlin, 1961.
C.L. Frommel, *Baldassare Peruzzi als Maler und Zeichner*, Vienna, 1967-1968.

15 G. Vasari, *Les vies des meilleurs peintres, sculpteurs et architectes*, edited by André Chastel, Paris, 1984, Vol. 6, p. 29.

16 Serlio, *I sette libri dell'architettura*, Book IV, chapter XI, Bologna, 1978.

17 L.B. Alberti, *L'architettura*, Book XI, chapter IV, Milan, 1966, p. 802.

18 J. Akerman, ''Sources of the Renaissance Villa,'' *Acts of the XXth International Congress of the History of Art: Studies in Western Art*, Vol. 2, Princeton, 1963.

19 P. Ogetti, *Palladio, Veronese e Vittoria a Maser*, Milan, 1960.
K. Oberhuber, ''Gli affreschi di Paolo Veronese nella Villa Barbaro,'' *Bollettino del Centro internazionale di studi di architettura Andrea Palladio*, X, 1968, p. 188.
J. Schulz, ''Le fonti di Paolo Veronese come decoratore,'' *idem*, p. 241.

20 W. Wolters, ''Andrea Palladio e la decorazione dei suoi edifici,'' *Bollettino del Centro... Andrea Palladio*, X, 1968, p. 255.

21 Vitruvius, *Les dix livres d'architecture*, edited by André Dalmas, Paris, 1979, p. 225. English translation, *On Architecture*, Loeb, London and Cambridge, Mass., 1931-1934.

22 B. Rupprecht, ''L'iconologia nella villa veneta,'' *Bollettino del Centro internazionale di studi di architettura Andrea Palladio*, X, 1968, p. 188.

23 A. Palladio, *Les quatre livres d'architecture*, French translation by Fréart de Chambray, Paris, 1980, p. 115.

24 T. Pugliatti, *Agostino Tassi: tra conformismo e libertà*, Rome, 1978.

25 We can see nothing ''grotesque'' in this decoration, as does I. Sjöström, *Quadratura*, Stockholm, 1978, p. 51.

26 T. Pugliatti (see above, note 24) expressed regret at seeing the doors of the Tassi room closed since 1969. We had the good fortune to gain access to Tassi's frescoes in the Palazzo Lancellotti ai Coronari. Tassi's landscapes are to be found on the ground floor of the palace, in the fifth room. We are most

grateful to Prince Pietro Lancellotti for allowing us to visit and photograph both the great hall and his private apartments.

27 This is probably one of the very first representations of a monumental, unhistoriated landscape.

28 These are *quadri riportati* represented in the form of a "picture within the picture."
See M. Milman, *Trompe-l'œil Painting*, Geneva, New York, London, 1982, p. 58.

29 E. Feinblatt, "Contributions to Girolamo Curti," *The Burlington Magazine*, CXVII, 1975, p. 342.

30 C.C. Malvasia, *Felsina pittrice. Vite de' pittori bolognesi*, edited by M. Barcaglia, Bologna, 1971, pp. 572-579. Malvasia emphasizes the debt of Colonna and Mitelli to Euclid and Vitruvius.

31 K.A. Piacenti, "The Summer Apartment of the Grand Duke," *Apollo*, 106, 1977, p. 190.

32 S. Sandström, *Levels of Unreality*, Uppsala, 1963, p. 173.

33 F.M. Aliberti Gaudioso and E. Gaudioso, "Sala Paolina" in *Gli affreschi di Paolo III a Castel Sant'Angelo 1543-1548. Progetto ed esecuzione*, exhibition catalogue, Museo Nazionale di Castel Sant'Angelo, Rome, 16 November 1981-31 January 1982, Vol. 2, p. 104.

34 F. Deuchler, *Duccio*, Milan, 1984.

35 Attention has only recently been focused on the drawing of the staircase and grotesques, on the back of the sketch representing the servants. By drawing on the back of the sheet, the artist was able to make an exact copy, by transparency, of the staircase and frescoes which actually existed in the Pompeian Corridor.

36 *Le opere di Giorgio Vasari*, edited by Gaetano Milanesi, Florence, 1906, Vol. 6, p. 679.

37 Quoted in P. Barocchi, *Vasari pittore*, Milan, 1964, p. 29.

38 For an exhaustive study of Salviati's frescoes and insight into the meaning of Mannerism in painting, see C. Dumont, *Francesco Salviati au Palais Sacchetti de Rome et la décoration murale italienne, 1520-1560*, Rome, 1973.

39 The "relation of uncertainty" *(relation d'incertitude)* is an expression coined by Marcel Raymond, *La poésie française et le maniérisme*, Geneva, 1971, p. 22. Quoted by C. Dumont, op. cit., p. 5.
G. Vasari, French edition of the *Lives* by André Chastel, Paris, 1984, Vol. 5, p. 19.

40 The front of the castle of Füssen is an example.
C. Klemm, "Edificio – architettura – pittura: soluzioni estreme nelle facciate dipinte tedesche fra gotico e barocco," *Facciate dipinte, conservazione e restauro. Atti del convegno di studi*, Genoa, 15-17 April 1982, p. 20.
M. Baur-Heinhold, *Bemalte Fassaden, Geschichte, Vorbild, Technik, Erneuerung*, Munich, 1975.

41 A. Marabottini, *Polidoro da Caravaggio*, Rome, 1969.
The grotesques in chiaroscuro in the castle at Civita Castellana are attributed by Nicole Dacos to Ripanda. The technique used by Ripanda combines *sgraffito* (scratchwork) with chiaroscuro, as described by Vasari.
N. Dacos, *La découverte de la Domus Aurea et la formation des grotesques à la Renaissance*, London, 1969, p. 80.
G. Vasari, edited by A. Chastel, Paris, 1984, Vol. 1, p. 180.

42 *Le opere di Giorgio Vasari*, edited by Milanesi, Florence, 1906, Vol. 5, p. 5, and Vol. 7, p. 497.

43 The façade of the Fondaco dei Tedeschi in Venice, now largely lost, was considered a masterpiece by contemporaries.

44 E. Panofsky, "Two Façades by Domenico Beccafumi," *Meaning in the Visual Arts*, New York, 1957, p. 234.

45 P. Boccardo, "L'esordio della facciata dipinta nelle ville genovesi del Cinquecento: rapporti tra committenza e iconografie," *Facciate dipinte, conservazione e restauro. Atti del convegno di studi*, Genoa, 15-17 April 1982, p. 243, note 12.

46 Rustic work "is very agreeable to the eye and represents in itself a sign of force" (Serlio), quoted by E. Gombrich, "Il palazzo del Te. Riflessioni su un mezzo secolo di fortuna critica: 1932-1982," *Quaderni di Palazzo Te*, 1, July-December 1984, p. 18.

47 P. Boccardo: see above, note 45.

48 The Golden Dachl house at Innsbruck, built about 1500 for Maximilian I, is decorated with a fresco whose iconography is similar.

49 Serlio, *I sette libri dell'architettura*, Book IV, chapter XI, p. 191.
Colonna and Mitelli painted the same "transparent form" on the inner courtyard façade of the Palazzo Este at Sassuolo when, in 1646, they tried with their frescoes to transform the medieval fortress into an agreeable residence. See *Restauri a Sassuolo*, Soprintendenza per i beni ambientali e architettonici dell'Emilia, Sassuolo, 1982.

50 The Ambras façade was painted from prints by Virgil Solis.
G. von Schlosser, *Raccolte d'arte e di meraviglie del tardo Rinascimento*, Florence, 1974, p. 55 ff.
E. Schlumberg, "Ambras," *Connaissance des Arts*, 183, 1967, p. 109.

51 Renaissance artists and archaeologists regarded the empty niche as an architectural element of ancient Rome. Moreover, the niches of Bramante's tempietto were not intended to house statues.
I. Gesche, *Neuaufstellungen antiker Statuen und ihr Einfluss auf die römische Renaissance-Architektur*, dissertation, Mannheim, 1971, p. 81.

52 C. Klemm, "Edificio – architettura – pittura: soluzioni estreme nelle facciate dipinte tedesche fra gotico e barocco," *Facciate dipinte, conservazione e restauro. Atti del convegno di studi*, Genoa, 15-17 April 1982, p. 21.

53 D. Koepplin, "Ausgeführte und entworfene Hausfassadenmalereien von Holbein, Stimmer und Bock: Kunsthybris mit dem erhobenen Zeigefinger," in the exhibition catalogue *Tobias Stimmer 1539-1584*, Basel, 28 September-9 December 1984, p. 55.

54 M.D. Fierro Morozzo della Rocca, "Rapporti tra architettura dipinta e strutture negli edifici genovesi dal Rinascimento al Novecento," *Facciate dipinte, conservazione e restauro. Atti del convegno di studi*, Genoa, 15-17 April 1982, pp. 223-227.

55 Serlio, *I sette libri dell'architettura*, Book IV, chapter XI, p. 191.

Chapter 3 (page 51)

1 E. Feinblatt, "Jesuit Ceiling Decoration," *The Art Quarterly*, 10, 1947, p. 237.
F. Haskell, *Patrons and Painters. Art and Society in Baroque Italy*, New Haven and London, 1980, p. 89 ff.

2 P. Seewaldt, *Giovanni Francesco Marchini. Sein Beitrag zur Monumentalmalerei des Spätbarocks in Deutschland*, Egelsbach, 1984.
The author is grateful to Dr Peter Seewaldt for kindly supplying the photographs used here to illustrate the work of Giovanni Francesco Marchini.

3 B. Rupprecht, *Die Brüder Asam: Sinn und Sinnlichkeit im bayerischen Barock*, Regensburg, 1980.

4 A. de Broglie, "Sabbioneta, une Brasilia au XVIe siècle," *Connaissance des Arts*, 268, June 1974, p. 107.

5 T. Poensgen, *Die Deckenmalerei in italienischen Kirchen*, Berlin, 1969, p. 76.

6 Barberini manuscript (MS lat. 6380), Vatican Library, quoted by E. Feinblatt, "The Roman Work of Domenico Maria Canuti," *The Art Quarterly*, XV, 1952, p. 45.

7 See MS Cod. Palat. 565, Biblioteca Nazionale, Florence: F. Baldinucci, *Vita del Padre Pozzo*, quoted by F. Haskell, *Patrons and Painters*, New Haven and London, 1980, p. 90.

8 Ingrid Sjöström, *Quadratura: Studies in Italian Ceiling Painting*, Stockholm, 1978, p. 63.

9 Gospel According to St Luke xii.49.

10 B. Kerber, *Andrea Pozzo*, Berlin and New York, 1971, p. 102 ff.

Notes and References

11 On the importance of the "centre" in symbolism and religion, see M. Eliade, *Images et symboles. Essais sur le symbolisme magico-religieux*, Paris, 1952, p. 37.

12 G. Flossmann and W. Hilger, *Stift Melk und seine Kunstschätze*, St Pölten, n.d.
G. Bazin, *Les palais de la foi*, Fribourg, 1981, p. 91.

13 H. Geiger, *Perspektivprobleme süddeutscher Deckenmalerei des Spät-barocks*, dissertation, Freiburg im Breisgau, 1953.

14 The emperors had their apartments in the buildings of the monastery.

15 M. Fagiolo, "L'universo della luce nell'idea di architettura del Vittone," *Bernardo Vittone e la disputa fra Classicismo e Barocco nel Settecento. Atti del convegno internazionale... nella ricordanza del secondo centenario della morte di B. Vittone*, Turin, 1972.

16 W. Oechslin, "Vittone e l'architettura europea del suo tempo," in *Bernardo Vittone... Atti del convegno...*, Turin, 1972.

17 R. Wittkower, "Vittone's Domes," *Studies in the Italian Baroque*, London, 1975.

18 R. Pommer, *Eighteenth-Century Architecture in Piedmont. The Open Structures of Juvarra, Alfieri, and Vittone*, New York, 1967.

19 Bernardo Vittone, *Instruzioni diverse*, Lugano, 1766, p. 183, quoted by W. Oechslin, see above, note 16.

20 R. Wittkower, *Idea and Image. Studies in the Italian Renaissance*, London, 1978, p. 175.

21 E. Gavazza, *La grande decorazione a Genova*, Genoa, 1974, p. 251 ff.

22 B. Kerber, *Andrea Pozzo*, Berlin and New York, 1971, p. 50.

23 L. Duclaux, "La décoration de la Chapelle de l'Hospice des Enfants-Trouvés," *Revue de l'Art*, 14, 1971, p. 45.

24 Gospel According to St Luke ii.13.

25 Among the subscribers figure the names of Watelet, Caylus and Madame de Pompadour.

Chapter 4 (page 67)

1 The medieval play took place in mansions or on trestle stages.
L. Magagnato, *Teatri italiani del Cinquecento*, Venice, 1954.
A. Chastel, "Les vues urbaines et le théâtre," *Bollettino del Centro internazionale di studi di architettura Andrea Palladio*, XVI, 1974.

2 A. Chastel, "Le lieu de la fête," *Fables, Formes, Figures*, I, Paris, 1978, p. 425.

3 N. Gabrielli, *L'arte nell'antico marchesato di Saluzzo*, Istituto Bancario San Paolo di Torino, Turin, 1973.

4 H. Demoriane, "La décoration et l'apparat de Condé-en-Brie dus au sens théâtral de Servandoni et Jean-Baptiste Oudry dans le château du comte de Sade," *Connaissance des Arts*, 179, January 1967, p. 37.

5 Quite in the spirit of the light-hearted dalliance of this decoration is the inscription beneath the entwined pair of Proserpine and Hades: "Proserpine, fear not a god beguiled by your charms."

6 G. Briganti, *Il Palazzo del Quirinale*, Rome, 1962.
S. Jacob, "Pierre de Cortone et la décoration de la galerie d'Alexandre VII au Quirinal," *Revue de l'Art*, 11, 1971, pp. 42-54.

7 The decoration of the Escalier des Ambassadeurs at Versailles no longer exists. It was painted from Le Brun's designs by Bonnemer, Houasse, Van der Meulen and others. While for this grand staircase Le Brun took over the iconography of Tassi and Lanfranco, he also resorted to the devices of Colonna who had just visited Paris.
See M.A. Schnapper, "Colonna et la 'Quadratura' en France à l'époque de Louis XIV," *Bulletin de la Société d'Histoire de l'Art Français*, 1966, p. 65.

8 K.A. Piacenti draws attention to the inventories of the period which show how little furniture there was in the audience chamber of Palazzo Pitti. Logi-cally enough, for a room transformed by simulated architecture does not support the presence of furniture against the walls.
K.A. Piacenti, "The Summer Apartment of the Grand Dukes," *Apollo*, 106, 1977, p. 190.

9 E. Lanners and P. and W. Studer, "Alles nur Schein," *Schweiz*, March 1983, p. 22.

10 J.J. Gloton, *Renaissance et Baroque à Aix-en-Provence*, 2, Rome, 1979, p. 258 ff.

11 The boy in the window recalls the "niche pieces" *(nisstuk)* of contemporary Dutch masters like Honthorst and Dou.

12 A. Venturi, "Affreschi nella delizia estense di Sassuolo," *L'Arte*, XX, 1917. See also: *Restauri a Sassuolo. Il Palazzo Ducale e la Piazza Garibaldi. Immagine storica e proposte di recupero*, Sassuolo, 1982.

13 The painted ornaments and architectures in the gallery are attributed to Giacomo Monti and Baldassarre Bianchi, the landscapes to Oliviero Delfino, the birds, fruit and flowers to Pier Francesco Cittadini. The overall design and figures are the work of Boulanger.

14 Boulanger here takes over the idea of simulated tapestries "lifted up" by human beings, like those painted by Domenichino at the beginning of the seventeenth century in the Villa Aldobrandini at Frascati (now in the National Gallery, London).

15 Fausto Lechi plausibly attributes these very fine transparent architectures in the Brescia villa to Antonio Galli Bibiena.
F. Lechi, *Le dimore bresciane in cinque secoli di storia*, 8, Brescia, p. 38 (272), note 18.
M. Marangoni, *I Carloni*, Florence, 1925.

16 See F. Lechi, op. cit., p. 27 (261).

17 R. Bossaglia, *I fratelli Galliari pittori*, Milan, 1962.
R. Bossaglia, "Riflessioni sui quadraturisti del Settecento lombardo," *La Critica d'Arte*, 42, 1960, p. 337.

18 G. Biavati, "Tre progetti autografi di Antonio Bibiena e le loro realizzazioni pittoriche," *Bollettino dei Musei civici genovesi*, I, July 1979, p. 23.

19 R. Pommer, *Eighteenth-Century Architecture in Piedmont. The Open Structures of Juvarra, Alfieri, and Vittone*, New York, 1967.

20 *Villa e Paese. Dimore nobili del Tuscolo e di Marino*, catalogue by Almamaria Tantillo Mignosi, Rome, 1980, pp. 96-100.

21 S. Bandes, "Gaspard Dughet's Frescoes in Palazzo Colonna, Rome," *The Burlington Magazine*, CXXIII, 1981, p. 77.

22 This is one of the first large-scale continuous landscapes that we know of.
M. Roethlisberger, "The Colonna Frescoes of Pietro Tempesta," *The Burlington Magazine*, CIX, 1967, pp. 12-16.
M. Roethlisberger, *Cavalier Tempesta and His Time*, Haarlem, 1970, pp. 38-41.

23 In this cell at Trinità dei Monti, Clérisseau seems to have taken over the idea of Natoire, who transformed the Chapelle des Innocents in Paris into a ruined cottage. See chapter 3, p. 64.
T.J. McCormick and J. Fleming, "A Ruin Room of Clérisseau," *The Connoisseur*, 1, 1962, p. 239.

24 See M. Roethlisberger, *Cavalier Tempesta and His Time*, Haarlem, 1970, p. 242 and note 7.

25 The taste of the Friars Minim for "strange" paintings appears again in their choice of an anamorphosis to decorate a corridor in the monastery of Trinità dei Monti (1642).

26 The drawing-room frescoes in the Casa Ferrari-Cartolari, Verona, are the work of Antonio Bibiena, who "invented" them, Filippo Maccari who worked out the designs, Lorenzo Pavia who did the painting, and Francesco Lorenzi who did the figures. See G. Biavati, "Tre progetti autografi di Antonio Bibiena e le loro realizzazioni pittoriche," *Bollettino dei Musei civici genovesi*, I, July 1979.

27 D. Gontard, "Scène de fête en Bohême," *Connaissance des Arts*, 367, September 1982, p. 82.

Chapter 5 (page 89)

1 Piranesi, *Diverse maniere*, quoted in J. Scott, *Piranesi*, London, 1975, p. 224.

2 Archives départementales ADS 1 FS 2634, "Convention entre le Conseil de fabrique de la métropole de Chambéry et M. Vicario pour les peintures à exécuter à la métropole de cette ville," 1833.

3 *Courrier des Alpes*, 16 February 1847.
The author is grateful to the keepers of the Musée Savoisien at Chambéry for kindly placing at her disposal the documents referred to in notes 2 and 3.

4 E.A. Entwhistle, *A Literary History of Wallpaper*, London, 1960.

5 Aldrophe report of 1867, quoted in J.P. Seguin, "Trois siècles de papiers peints," in the exhibition catalogue *Des siècles de papiers peints*, Musée des Arts Décoratifs, Paris, 22 June-15 October 1967.

6 Richard Morris Hunt (1827-1895), an American architect of international standing, worked both in the United States and France.
P.F. Michel, *Glasmalerei um 1900 in der Schweiz*, Liestal, 1985.
L. Lee, G. Seddon, F. Stephen, *Stained Glass*, London, 1976.

7 First suggested by a German architectural painter named Breisig, the panoramas were patented in 1787 by Robert Barker, who exhibited one in his native Edinburgh in 1788. The first Rotunda was built in London in 1801 by Mitchell.
See S. Oettermann, *Das Panorama. Die Geschichte eines Massenmediums*, Frankfurt am Main, 1980.

8 *Zeitschrift für Schweizerische Archäologie und Kunstgeschichte*, 42, 1985, Heft 4, with review of the colloquy *Das Panorama* held in Lucerne, 25-27 April 1985.

9 After the Franco-Prussian War of 1870, military panoramas became very popular.
See F. Robichon, "Emotion et sentiment dans les panoramas militaires après 1870," in op. cit. above, note 8, p. 281.

10 The device was invented by Daguerre and Bouton, who in 1822 opened the first Diorama in Paris.
See H. and A. Gernsheim, *L.J.M. Daguerre. The History of the Diorama and the Daguerreotype*, New York, 1968.

11 In the press of the period one notes the phrases which since antiquity have been used to express the reactions of viewers "fooled" by a trompe-l'œil painting. Describing one of the most popular dioramas, "The Chapel of Holyrood Castle," displayed in Paris in 1823 and in London in 1825, the article published in *The Mirror of Literature* (26 March 1825) says: "The stars are shining in their sphere, sometimes obscured, sometimes emerging from the clouds, while the moon glides imperceptibly, sometimes under the haze, sometimes in a clear sky, and the light reflected by the walls, shafts and broken architraves becomes subdued or bright... So then, if this is painting, of however exquisite a kind, it is something more; for the elements move while the illuminated objects are motionless." Quoted in op. cit., note 10 above, pp. 26-27.

12 M.D. Fierro Morozzo della Rocca, "Rapporti tra architettura dipinta e struttura negli edifici genovesi dal Rinascimento al Novecento," *Facciate dipinte, conservazione e restauro. Atti del convegno di studi*, Genoa, 15-17 April 1982, p. 224.

13 Down to the present day, some taxes in Italy are calculated according to the number of windows on the street. To produce an impression of wealth, at low cost, they were often replaced by painted windows.
On painted house-fronts in the Germanic lands, see M. Baur-Heinhold, *Bemalte Fassaden, Geschichte, Vorbild, Technik, Erneuerung*, Munich, 1975.

14 Lise Grenier and Hans Wiese Benedetti, "Ville et théâtre," in *Le siècle de l'éclectisme. Lille 1830-1930*, collective work, Paris - Brussels, 1979.

15 B. Zevi, "Contro il neo-accademismo," *Casabella*, 1981, p. 471.

16 *L'art public*, collective work, Paris, 1981.

17 G. Hesse, *Gemalte Illusionen. Wandbilder in Berlin*, Dortmund, 1983.

18 Quoted in D. Durand and D. Boulogne, *Le livre du mur peint. Art et techniques*, Paris, 1984, p. 24.

19 Richard Haas, *An Architecture of Illusion*, New York, 1981, p. 84.
The mural for the Boston Architectural Center in Newbury Street was commissioned by the National Paint and Coatings Association, coordinated by City Walls, Inc., and executed by Seaboard Outdoor Advertising.

20 For a good study of the influence of the Panorama on late nineteenth and early twentieth century architecture, see S. Malfroy, "Extensions de l'illusionnisme du panorama dans l'architecture privée," in op. cit., note 8 above, p. 331.

21 Delvaux's fresco is in the Maison Perrier in Brussels. Dali's painted ceiling is in the Palais Alleusis in Barcelona.

22 E. Panofsky, "Die Perspektive als symbolische Form," *Vorträge der Bibliothek Warburg*, 1924-1925. Quoted from the French translation of this famous essay, *La perspective comme forme symbolique*, Paris, 1975, p. 39.

23 Interview with Paolini in *Libération*, 19 June 1985.

24 For other connections between Paolini's work and perspective theory, see Laurent Busine, *Les doublures de Giulio Paolini*, Brussels, 1986.

25 Private communication from Felice Varini.

26 Y.A. Bois, "Avatars de l'axonométrie," *Images et imaginaires d'architecture*, exhibition catalogue, Centre Georges Pompidou, Paris, 8 March-28 May 1984, p. 129.

The author would like to thank the following for their kind welcome: Prince Pietro Lancellotti, Rome; Marchese Giulio Sacchetti, Rome; Dr Barina and the Administration of the Palazzo del Quirinale, Rome; the Administration of the Palazzo Pallavicini-Rospigliosi, Rome; the Administration of the Palazzo Colonna, Rome; Dr Kirsten Piacenti, Director of the Museo degli Argenti, Palazzo Pitti, Florence; Signora Renata Verita Poeta, Verona; and Monsieur Alain Paste de Rochefort, Condé-en-Brie.

List of Illustrations

ALBERTI Cherubino (1553-1618) and Giovanni (1558-1601): Sacristy, Basilica of St John Lateran, Rome, 1592. (Photo Cuchi White, Paris) 30

ALDROVANDINI Pompeo (1677-c. 1735): Ceiling painting, Palazzo Doria-Pamphili, Rome, 1734-1735. (Photos Miriam Milman) 6-7

ALTICHIERO (c. 1320-c. 1385): Chapel of San Jacopo, Basilica of Sant'Antonio, Padua, 1374-1376. (Photo Gérard Zimmermann, Geneva) 17

ANNECY: Church of St Maurice, 1458. (Photo Cuchi White, Paris) 15

ANSALDO Giovanni Andrea (1584-1638): Villa Negrone, Prà, near Genoa, 1630. (Photo Cuchi White, Paris) 35

ARBAUDI Costanzo (died 1657) and Francesco (died after 1661): Courtyard, Maresco Castle, near Saluzzo, Piedmont, 1613-1623. (Photo Cuchi White, Paris) 68

ASAM Cosmas Damian (1686-1739): Descent of the Holy Ghost, Benedictine Abbey Church of St Martin and St Oswald, Weingarten, Baden-Württemberg, 1718. (Photo Wolf Christian von der Mulbe, Dachau) 54

— Descent of the Holy Ghost, Cistercian Abbey Church of the Assumption (Mariä Himmelfahrt), St John the Baptist and St Ursula, Aldersbach (Passau), Bavaria, 1720. (Photo Wolf Christian von der Mulbe, Dachau) 55

BALDANCOLI Pietro (1834-1901): Drawing-room, Palazzo Serristori, Florence, 1896-1897. (Photo Cuchi White, Paris) 90

BENSO Giulio (1601-1668): Preparatory drawing for the hall decoration, Château Grimaldi, 1648. Pen and ink. (12½ × 8⅝ in.) Graphische Sammlung, Staatsgalerie, Stuttgart, Inv. 6234. (Museum Photo) 36

— Hall decoration, Château Grimaldi, Cagnes-sur-Mer, 1648. (Photo Cuchi White, Paris) 37

— Annunciation, Church of the Santissima Annunziata del Vastato, Genoa, 1638. (Photo Cuchi White, Paris) 64

BIBIENA Antonio Galli (1700-1774): Chapel of the Holy Sacrament, Assunta Church, Sabbioneta (Mantua), 1773. (Photo P. Hinous, Connaissance des Arts/Edimedia, Paris) 56

BIBIENA Antonio Galli (1700-1774) and collaborators: Drawing-room, Casa Ferrari-Cartolari, Verona, 1765. (Photos Gérard Zimmermann, Geneva) 80, 87

BIBIENA Giuseppe Galli (1696-1756): Setting for the Theatrum Sacrum of the Court Chapel in Vienna, 1740. From Giuseppe Galli Bibiena, *Architectural and Perspective Designs*, Dover Publications, New York, 1964 68

— "Magnificent Place," sketch, early 18th century. Staatliche Graphische Sammlung, Munich. (Archive Photo) 79

BOCK THE ELDER Hans (c. 1550/1552-1624): Façade design, 1571. Pen and ink wash. (19½ × 15½ in.) Print Room, Öffentliche Kunstsammlung, Basel, Inv. U.IV.65. (Museum Photo) 50

List of Illustrations

BOLZANO, Roncolo Castle (Burg Runkelstein): Stua da bagno (bathroom), late 14th century. (Photos M. Pintarelli, Museo Civico, Bolzano) 22-23

BORIANI Davide (1936): Architecture of the past, Pavia, 1975. (Photo Cuchi White, Paris) 98

BOULANGER Master (mid-17th century): Palazzo d'Este, Sassuolo (Modena), 1646. (Photo Cuchi White, Paris) 85

BOULANGER Master (mid-17th century) and collaborators: Gallery, Palazzo d'Este, Sassuolo (Modena), 1646. (Photo Miriam Milman) 75

BRUNETTI, see NATOIRE.

CAMPI Antonio (died c. 1591): Church of San Paolo, Milan, 1588. (Photo Cuchi White, Paris) 34

CANUTI Domenico Maria (1620-1684) and Enrico HAFFNER (1640-1702): Glory of St Dominic, Church of SS. Domenico e Sisto, Rome, 1674. (Photo Cuchi White, Paris) 57

CARLONE Carlo (1686-1775): Detail of the drawing-room, villa near Brescia, 1745. (Photo Cuchi White, Paris) 87

CARLONE Carlo (1686-1775), Giacomo LECCHI (mid-18th century) and collaborators: Drawing-room, villa near Brescia, 1745. (Photos Cuchi White, Paris). 76-77

CLÉRISSEAU Charles Louis (1722-1820): Monastery of Trinità dei Monti, Rome, 1766. (Photos Cuchi White, Paris) 83

COLONNA Angelo Michele (1600-1687) and Agostino MITELLI (1609-1660): Audience Chamber, Palazzo Pitti, Museo degli Argenti, Florence, 1636-1641. (Photos Cuchi White, Paris) 42-43, 72

DAGUERRE Jacques (1787-1851): Ruins of Holyrood Chapel, Edinburgh, 1824. Oil on canvas after his Diorama subject. (83 × 101 in.) Walker Art Gallery, Liverpool. (Museum Photo) . . . 93

DARET Pierre (1604-1678): Hôtel de Châteaurenard, Aix-en-Provence, 1654. (Photo Cuchi White, Paris) 73

FANTI, see ROTTMAYR.

FLORENCE: Wedding, Chamber, Palazzo Davanzati, 1395. (Photos Cuchi White, Paris). 20-21

FLORENCE: Scrittoio del Terrazzo (Terrace Study or Office), Palazzo della Signoria (Palazzo Vecchio), Florence, about 1562. (Photo Cuchi White, Paris) 26

GALLIARI Bernardino (1707-1794) and Fabrizio (1709-1790): Drawing-room, Villa Crivelli, Castellazzo di Bollate (Milan), 1752. (Photo Cuchi White, Paris) 78

— Festival Hall, Château des Marches, near Chambéry (Savoy), 1785-1790. (Photo Cuchi White, Paris) 79

GENTILESCHI, see TASSI.

GHEZZI Pier Leone (1674-1755): Parlour (Stanza delle Conversazioni), Villa Falconieri, Frascati (Rome), 1727. (Photo Cuchi White, Paris). 86

GIOTTO (1266-1337) and his workshop: Upper Church of San Francesco, Assisi, early 14th century. (Photo Cuchi White, Paris) 17

GOTHIC WORKSHOP: Frescoes in the transept and choir, Upper Church of San Francesco, Assisi, late 13th century. (Photo Cuchi White, Paris). 14

GRANVELLE Philippe (1954). Visions, 1980. (Photo by courtesy of the artist) 102

GRIMALDI Giovanni Francesco (1608-1680): Hall of Spring, Villa Falconieri, Frascati (Rome), 1672. (Photo Cuchi White, Paris) 82

HAAS Richard (1936): West façade, Boston Architectural Center, Newbery Street, Boston, 1975-1977. (50 × 78 ft.) Commissioned by National Paint and Coatings Association; coordinated by City Walls, Inc.; executed by Seaboard Outdoor Advertising. (Photo Georg Gerster, Zumikon-Zürich) 96

HAFFNER, see CANUTI.

HUNT Richard Morris (1827-1895): Stained-glass window designed by Hunt and executed in Paris by E.S. Oudinot, 1883-1884. From the home of Henry Gurdon Marquand (1819-1902) at 11 East 68th Street, New York. Gift of Miss Susan Dwight Bliss, Museum of the City of New York. (Photo Cuchi White, Paris). 92

ISSOGNE CASTLE (Valley of Aosta), Sala Baronale: View of Jerusalem and Golgotha, 15th century. Courtesy Associazione fra le Casse di Risparmio Italiane, Rome. (Photo Mario Carrieri) 18

JUVARA Filippo (1676-1736): Hunting Lodge of Stupinigi, Piedmont, with painted decoration by the Valeriani brothers, 1733. (Photos Cuchi White, Paris). 61, 81

LANFRANCO, see TASSI.

LANOUVELLE, see RENTY.

LE BRUN Charles (1619-1690): Grand Staircase or Escalier des Ambassadeurs, Versailles, 1676-1678. Print by Surugue. Cabinet des Estampes, Bibliothèque Nationale, Paris. (Photo BN) 72

LECCHI, see CARLONE.

LEDERER Josef (mid-18th century): Self-Portrait with Cup of Coffee, Hall of Masks, Castle of Česky-Krumlov, Czechoslovakia, 1748. (Photo Denis Gontard, Aix-en-Provence) . . 86

LEWITT Sol (1928): Forms Derived from a Cube. Isometric figures drawn in colour and India ink washes with a six-inch ink wash border. First installation: John Weber Gallery, New York, December 1982. Courtesy of John Weber Gallery, New York. (Photo Fred Scruton). 101

MAIENFELD (Grisons, Switzerland): Salenegg Castle, 1782. (Photo Miriam Milman) 73

MANTEGNA Andrea (1431-1506): Camera degli Sposi (Wedding Chamber), Ducal Palace, Mantua, 1461-1474. (Photo © Michel Desjardins, Agence Top, Paris) 28-29

MARCHINI Giovanni Francesco (early 18th century): Heilig-Kreuz Chapel, Church of Sankt Jakob, Wiesentheid, Franconia, 1730. (Photo Dr. Peter Seewaldt, Trierweiler) 53

MENGOZZI-COLONNA, see TIEPOLO.

MITCHELL Robert (active 1782-1801): Section of the Rotunda in Leicester Square, London, with Robert Barker's Panorama paintings, 1801. Aquatint. (12¾ × 18½ in.) Kunstbibliothek mit Museum für Architektur, Modebild und Grafik-Design, Staatliche Museen Preussischer Kulturbesitz, West Berlin. (Museum Photo) 93

MITELLI, see COLONNA.

MORAZZONE II (c. 1571-1626) and TANZIO DA VARALLO (1576- c.1655): Ecce Homo Chapel, Church of Sacro Monte, Varallo, Piedmont, 1609. (Photo Scala, Florence) 63

NATOIRE Charles (1700-1777), Gaetano BRUNETTI (died 1758) and Paolo Antonio BRUNETTI (1723-1783): Chapel of the Hospice des Enfants-Trouvés, Paris, 1751. Print by Etienne Fessard after Augustin de Saint-Aubin. Cabinet des Estampes, Bibliothèque Nationale, Paris. (Photo BN) 66

NEUHAUS Gert (1939): Opening Zipper, painted wall in West Berlin, 1979. (39½ × 59 ft.) Wohnbau-Gesellschaft Krogmann, Berlin. (Photo Der Senator für Bau- und Wohnungswesen, Berlin-Wilmersdorf) 94

PAOLINI Giulio (1940): De Pictura (On Painting), 1979. Collage of nine canvases, pencil and photographic fragments. (8 × 12 ft.) Staatsgalerie, Stuttgart. (Museum Photo) 99

PERIN DEL VAGA (c. 1501-1547): Decorative design for the north front, Palazzo Doria, Genoa. Pen and wash. Musée Condé, Chantilly. (Photo Giraudon, Paris) 48

PERIN DEL VAGA (c. 1501-1547) and Pellegrino TIBALDI (1527-1596): Sala Paolina or Council Hall, Castel Sant'Angelo, Rome, 1546-1547. (Photo Cuchi White, Paris) 44

PERUZZI Baldassarre (1481-1536): Hall of Perspectives, Villa Farnesina, Rome, about 1512. (Photo Cuchi White, Paris) . . 38

PIRANESI Giovan Battista (1720-1778): Wall decoration, English Coffee House, Piazza di Spagna, Rome. Print from his *Diverse maniere*, Rome, 1769 89

POLIDORO DA CARAVAGGIO (1495/1500-1546): Façade design, Palazzo Gaddi (demolished), Rome. Pen and bistre. Graphische Sammlung Albertina, Vienna, Inv. 15.462. (Photo Albertina) 47

POMPEII, Villa of the Mysteries: Frescoes, first century B.C. (Photos Skira Archives and Cuchi White, Paris) 8, 10

— Casa del Frutteto: Cubiculum floreale, before 79 A.D. (Photo Cuchi White, Paris) 11

— House of the Vettii: Room of Pentheus, first century A.D. (Photo Cuchi White, Paris) 13

POZZO Andrea (1642-1709): Painted dome, Church of Sant'Ignazio, Rome, 1685. (Photo Cuchi White, Paris) . . . 52

— Dome of the Collegio Romano, Rome. From *Perspectiva pictorum et architectorum*, Rome, 1737 52

— Glory of St Ignatius and the Society of Jesus, Church of Sant'Ignazio, Rome, 1688. (Photo Cuchi White, Paris) . . . 58

— Corridor of St Ignatius' rooms, Collegio Romano, Rome, 1682-1686. (Photo Cuchi White, Paris) 65

RAPHAEL (1483-1520) and his workshop: Vault decoration of the third dome in the Loggie, Vatican Palace, Rome, about 1517-1519. (Photo Scala, Florence) 32

RE Vincenzo (died 1762): Palazzo Reale, Portici (Naples), 18th century. (Photo Cuchi White, Paris) 74

RENTY Baudouin de (1957) and Philippe de LANOUVELLE (1957): Belle Epoque staircase, Paris, 1984. (Photo by courtesy of the artists) 98

RIETI Fabio (1925): Painted wall, Quai de Rive Neuve, Vieux-Port, Marseilles, May 1983. (Photo by the artist) 95

RIPANDA Giacomo (early 15th century): Courtyard vault, Castle of Civita Castellana (Viterbo), about 1500. Scratchwork and grisaille. (Photo Cuchi White, Paris) 47

ROME, Palatine Hill: House of the Griffins, first century B.C. (Photo Miriam Milman) 12

ROME: Church of San Saba, late 13th century. (Photo Cuchi White, Paris) 16

ROME, Palazzo del Quirinale: Sala Regia by Tassi and Lanfranco, 1616-1617 71

— Coffee House Pavilion, 18th century 84

— Hall of the Piedmontese Tapestries, late 19th century 88

(Photos Cuchi White, Paris)

ROSSI Gian Domenico (active 1755-1763): Church of the Confraternità della Misericordia, Saluzzo, Piedmont, 1763. (Photo Cuchi White, Paris) 62

ROTTMAYR Johann Michael (1654-1730) and Gaetano FANTI (1687-1759): Glory of St Benedict, Benedictine Abbey Church of Melk, Lower Austria, 1720-1721. (Photo Augustin Baumgartner, Graz) 59

RUBENS Peter Paul (1577-1640): Drawing of the façade, Palazzo Salvago, Genoa 50

List of Illustrations

SALVIATI Francesco (1510-1563): Palazzo Sacchetti, Rome, 1553-1554. (Photo Cuchi White, Paris)   46

SCAMOZZI Vincenzo (1552-1616): Olympic Theatre, Sabbioneta (Mantua), 1588. (Photo P. Hinous, Connaissance des Arts/Edimedia, Paris)   69

SEGA Giovanni del (died 1527): Hall of the Moors, Castle of Carpi (Modena), 1506. Museo Civico, Carpi. (Museum Photo)   19

SERLIO Sebastiano (1475-1554): Tragic Scene, stage design. Woodcut from his *Libro primo...d'architettura,* Venice, 1551, fol. 29 v.   67

SERVANDONI Giovanni Niccolò (1695-1766): Drawing-room, Château de Condé-en-Brie (Aisne), about 1740. (Photo Cuchi White, Paris).   71

SIGHIZZI Andrea (died 1684): Palazzo Reale, Genoa, 17th century. (Photo Cuchi White, Paris).   84

TANZIO DA VARALLO, see MORAZZONE.

TASSI Agostino (c. 1580-1644): Palazzo Lancellotti ai Coronari, Rome, 1617-1623. (Photos Cuchi White, Paris) 31, 41

TASSI Agostino (c. 1580-1644) and Orazio GENTILESCHI (1562-1647): Casino delle Muse, Palazzo Pallavicini-Rospigliosi, Rome, 1611-1612. (Photo Cuchi White, Paris)   40

TASSI Agostino (c. 1580-1644) and Giovanni LANFRANCO (1582-1647): Sala Regia (Royal Hall), Palazzo del Quirinale, Rome, 1616-1617. (Photo Cuchi White, Paris)   71

TEMPESTA Pietro (c. 1637-1701): Drawing-room, Palazzo Colonna, Rome, 1668. (Photos Cuchi White, Paris)   82

TEUFEL Heinrich (died 1570): Inner courtyard, Castle of Ambras, near Innsbruck, 1567-1568. (Photo Miriam Milman)   49

TIBALDI, see PERIN DEL VAGA.

TIEPOLO Giambattista (1696-1770) and Gerolamo MENGOZZI-COLONNA (c. 1688- c. 1772): Drawing-room, Palazzo Labia, Venice, 1747-1750. (Photo Cuchi White, Paris)   70

TRENTO: Palazzo Geremia, early 16th century. (Photo Gérard Zimmermann, Geneva)   49

VAISSEAU GROUP, Geneva, with the collaboration of Emmanuelle AMBROSETTI: Wall decoration, inner passage, Pélisserie building, Rue Frank Martin, Geneva, August-September 1983. (Photo J.F. Schlemmer, Geneva)   97

VARINI Felice (1952): View: Young Sculpture, Port of Austerlitz, Paris, May 1985. (Photo Antoine Deroux)   100

VASARI Giorgio (1511-1574): Hall of the Hundred Days or Large Council Hall, Palazzo della Cancelleria, Rome, 1546. (Photo Skira Archives)   45

VERONESE Paolo (1528-1588): Fresco, Stanza del Tribunale d'Amore, Villa Barbaro, Maser near Asolo (Treviso), Venetia, about 1560. (Photo Giacomelli, Venice)   39

— Fresco, Villa Barbaro, Maser, about 1560. (Photo Giacomelli, Venice)   103

VICARIO Casimir (early 19th century): Nave decoration, Chambéry Cathedral (Savoy), 1833. (Photo Cuchi White, Paris) . .   91

VITTONE Bernardo (1705-1770): Church of San Bernardino, Chieri, Piedmont, 1740-1744. (Photo Gérard Zimmermann, Geneva).   60

— Assunta Church, Riva di Chieri, Piedmont, 1766-1767. (Photo Gérard Zimmermann, Geneva).   60

— Church of Santa Chiara, Brà, Piedmont, 1742. (Photo Cuchi White, Paris).   61

WALLPAPER, 1835-1840. (19¼ × 22½ in.) Musée des Arts Décoratifs, Paris. Inv. 29553. (Photo L. Sully-Jaulmes)   92

WENZLAUS (?): Months of May, July and August, details, Eagle's Tower, Castle of Trento, about 1400. (Photos Gérard Zimmermann, Geneva) 24-25

WHITE Kenn: Painted façade, London, about 1979. (Photo Cuchi White, Paris).   94

ZUCCARI Federico (c. 1540-1609): Room of Ganymede, Palazzo Zuccari, Rome, before 1603. (Photo Giorgio Vasari, Rome)   33

Index of Names

ADAM Robert (1728-1792) and James (1730-1794) 83.

Aix-en-Provence, Châteaurenard House 73, 74.

ALBERTI Cherubino (1553-1618) and Giovanni (1558-1601) 30, 31, 33, 52.

ALBERTI Leon Battista (c. 1404-1472) 21, 37, 38, 99.

Aldersbach (Bavaria), Abbey Church 55.

ALDROVANDINI Pompeo (1677-c. 1735) 6, 7.

ALTICHIERO (c. 1320-c. 1385) 17.

ALTIERI Marc Antonio (1450-1532) 30.

Ambras Castle, Innsbruck 49, 50.

AMBROSETTI Emmanuelle 97.

ANDREA DEL SARTO (1486-1530) 48.

Annecy (Savoy), St-Maurice 15.

ANSALDO Giovanni Andrea (1584-1638) 35, 36.

ARBAUDI Costanzo (died 1657) and Francesco (died 1661) 68, 69.

ARETINO Pietro (1492-1556) 38.

ASAM Cosmas Damian (1686-1739) and Egid Quirin (1692-1750) 54, 55.

Assisi (Umbria), Upper Church of San Francesco 14-17.

BACCICI or BACICCIO, see GAULLI.

BALDANCOLI Pietro (1834-1901) 90.

BALDINUCCI Filippo (c. 1623-1696) 58.

BARBARO Daniele (1513-1570) 38, 39.

BARKER Robert (1739-1806) 92, 93.

BAUDRILLARD Jean 6.

BELLEGARDE Marquis de 78, 79.

BENSO Giulio (1601-1668) 36, 37, 64.

Berlin 94, 95.

BERNINI Gian Lorenzo (1598-1680) 52, 56, 57.

BIBIENA Antonio Galli (1700-1774) 56, 68, 77, 80, 86, 87, 98.

BIBIENA Giuseppe Galli (1696-1756) 68, 77, 79.

BOCK THE ELDER Hans (c. 1550/52-1624) 50.

Bolzano (South Tyrol), Roncolo Castle 22, 23.

BORGHESE Scipione (1576-1633) 40.

BORIANI Davide (1936) 98.

Boston Architectural Center 96.

BOULANGER, Master (mid-17th century) 75, 85.

BOULLÉE Etienne-Louis (1728-1799) 96.

Brà (Piedmont), Santa Chiara 61, 62.

Brescia 76, 77, 87.

BRUNETTI Gaetano (died 1758) and Paolo Antonio (1723-1783) 66.

Brussels, Perrier House 97.

Cagnes-sur-Mer, Château Grimaldi 36, 37.

CAMPI Antonio (died c. 1591) 34.

CANUTI Domenico Maria (1620-1684) 57.

CARLONE Carlo (1686-1775) 76, 77, 87, 97.

Carpi Castle, Emilia 19.

Castellazzo di Bollate (Lombardy), Villa Crivelli 78, 79.

Česky-Krumlov Castle (Burg Krummau), Bohemia 86.

Chambéry (Savoy), Château des Marches 78, 79;
Cathedral 91.

Chieri (Piedmont), San Bernardino 60, 61.

CHIRICO Giorgio de (1888-1978) 80.

Civita Castellana (Latium), Castle 47.

CLEMENT VIII, Pope (1592-1605) 31.

CLÉRISSEAU Charles-Louis (1722-1820) 83.

COLONNA Angelo Michele (1600-1687) 42, 43, 72, 73, 75.

Condé-en-Brie (Aisne), Château 70, 71.

CONSTANTINE THE GREAT (c. A.D. 280-337) 16.

CORREGGIO (c. 1489-1534) 31.

Cosmati inlay work 16.

CURTI Gerolamo (1570-1632) 42.

DAGUERRE Jacques (1787-1851) 92, 93.

DALI Salvador (1904) 97.

DARET Pierre (1604-1678) 73, 74, 97.

Delos, Greece 9.

DELVAUX Paul (1897) 97.

DIDEROT Denis (1713-1784) 83.

Dioramas 92, 93.

DORIA Andrea (1466-1560) 48.

DUCCIO (c. 1255-1319) 44.

Edinburgh, Scotland 92, 93.

ELEONORA OF TOLEDO (1522-1562) 26.

FANTI Gaetano (1687-1759) 58-60.

FERDINAND II of Tyrol (1529-1595) 49.

Florence 42, 48, 90, 97;
Baptistery 14;
Palazzo Davanzati 20, 21;
Palazzo Pitti 43, 72, 73;
Palazzo Serristori 90, 91;
Palazzo della Signoria 26.

Frascati (Latium), Villa Falconieri 82, 86, 87.

GALLIARI Bernardino (1707-1794) and Fabrizio (1709-1790) 78, 79.

GAULLI Giovan Battista (1639-1709) 57.

Geneva 97.

Genoa 36, 64, 65;
Palazzo Doria 48;
Palazzo Reale 84;
Palazzo Salvago 50;
Santissima Annunziata del Vastato 64, 65;
Villa Negrone 34.

Index of Names

GENTILESCHI Orazio (1562-1647) 40.
GHEZZI Pier Leone (1674-1755) 86.
GIORGIONE (1477-1510) 48.
GIOTTO (1266-1337) 17.
GONZAGA Francesco (1444-1483) 30.
GRANVELLE Philippe (1954) 102.
GRIMALDI Giovanni Francesco (1608-1680) 82.
GUARINI Guarino (1624-1683) 62.

HAAS Richard (1936) 96.
HAFFNER Enrico (1640-1702) 57, 59.
HUNT Richard Morris (1827-1895) 92.

IGNATIUS OF LOYOLA St (c. 1491-1556) 58, 59, 65.
Innsbruck (Austria), Ambras Castle 49, 50.
Issogne Castle (Aosta) 18, 19.

JACQUIER François (1711-1788) 83.
JEROME St (c. 347-419/420) 25.
JUVARA Filippo (1676-1736) 61, 62, 81.

LANFRANCO Giovanni (1582-1647) 71, 72.
LANOUVELLE Philippe de (1957) 98.
LE BRUN Charles (1619-1690) 72.
LECCHI Giacomo (mid-18th century) 76, 77.
LE CORBUSIER (1887-1965) 96.
LEDERER Josef (mid-18th century) 86.
LEDOUX Claude-Nicolas (1736-1806) 96.
LEONARDO DA VINCI (1452-1519) 31.
LEOPOLD III of Habsburg, Duke of Austria (died 1386) 23.
LESSING G.E. (1729-1781) 99.
LE SUEUR Thomas (1703-1770) 83.
LEWITT Sol (1928) 101.
LIECHTENSTEIN Georg von 25.
LIECHTENSTEIN Prince of 58.
London 93-95;
    Panorama Rotunda 93.

Madrid 42.
Maienfeld (Grisons), Salenegg Castle 73.
MALEVICH Kasimir (1878-1935) 101.
MALVASIA Carlo Cesare (1616-1693) 42.
MANTEGNA Andrea (1431-1506) 27-30, 97.
Mantua (Lombardy), Ducal Palace 27-30.
Marches, Château des (Chambéry) 78, 79.
MARCHINI Giovanni Francesco (18th century) 52, 53.
Maresco Castle (Piedmont) 68, 69.
Marseilles 95.
MARTINI Francesco di Giorgio (1439-1502) 30.
Maser (Venetia), Villa Barbaro 38, 39, 103.
MAXIMILIAN I (1459-1519) 48.
MEDICI, the 26, 43, 72.
Melk (Austria), Abbey Church 59, 60.

MENGOZZI-COLONNA Gerolamo (c. 1688-c. 1772) 70.
MENGS Anton Raphael (1728-1779) 83.
MICHELANGELO (1475-1564) 42, 44, 45.
MIES VAN DER ROHE Ludwig (1887-1969) 96.
Milan 78, 79;
    Sala delle Asse 31;
    San Paolo 34.
MITCHELL Robert (active 1782-1801) 93.
MITELLI Agostino (1609-1660) 42, 43, 72, 73, 75.
MODANINO II (17th century) 82.
MONTAIGNE (1533-1592) 50.
MORAZZONE II (Pier Francesco MAZZUCCHELLI, c. 1571-1626) 63.

NATOIRE Charles (1700-1777) 66, 83.
NERO (A.D. 37-68) 12.
NEUHAUS Gert (1939) 94, 95.
Nice 36.

OUDINOT Eugène Stanislas (1827-1889) 92.

Padua (Venetia), Sant'Antonio 17.
PALLADIO Andrea (1508-1580) 38, 39.
PANOFSKY Erwin (1892-1968) 27, 99.
Panoramas 92, 93.
PAOLINI Giulio (1940) 99.
Paris 42, 92, 93, 98, 100;
    Foundling Hospital 66;
    Panorama Rotunda 92.
Parma (Emilia), San Paolo convent 31.
PAUL III, Pope (1534-1549) 44, 45.
Pavia (Lombardy) 98.
PAVILLON Pierre 73.
PERIN DEL VAGA (c. 1501-1547) 44, 45, 48.
PERUZZI Baldassarre (1481-1536) 38, 44, 47, 68.
PETRARCH (1304-1374) 25, 26.
PHILIP THE BOLD (1342-1404) 15.
PIERO DI COSIMO (1462-1521) 26.
PIETRO DA CORTONA (1596-1669) 56.
PIRANESI Giovan Battista (1720-1778) 77, 89, 98.
PLINY THE ELDER (A.D. 38-79) 25.
PLINY THE YOUNGER (A.D. 62-c. 114) 25.
POLIDORO DA CARAVAGGIO (1495/1500-1546) 47.
Pompeii 9-14, 16;
    Casa del Frutteto 10, 11;
    House of the Vettii 12, 13, 16;
    Villa of the Mysteries 8-10.
Portici (Naples), Palazzo Reale 74.
POZZO Andrea (1642-1709) 51-53, 55, 58, 59, 65, 74.
Prà (Genoa), Villa Negrone 35.

Quadraturisti (painters of illusionist decorations) 42, 58, 67, 68, 90.

RAPHAEL (1483-1520) 32, 34, 38.
RE Vincenzo (died 1762) 74.
RENTY Baudouin de (1957) 98.
RIETI Fabio (1925) 95.
RIPANDA Giacomo (15th century) 47.
Riva di Chieri (Piedmont), Assunta Church 60, 61.
ROBBIA Luca II della (c. 1475-1550) 26.
Rome 9, 14, 34, 38, 46-48, 50, 51, 56, 82, 83, 90, 97;
    Castel Sant'Angelo 44, 45;
    Collegio Romano 53, 65;
    Domus Aurea 12;
    English Coffee House 89, 90;
    Farnesina House 14;
    Gesù (Chiesa del Gesù) 57;
    House of Augustus 14;
    House of the Griffins 12;
    Palazzo della Cancelleria 45;
    Palazzo Colonna 82;
    Palazzo Gaddi 47;
    Palazzo Lancellotti ai Coronari 31, 40, 41;
    Palazzo Pallavicini-Rospigliosi 40;
    Palazzo del Quirinale 71, 72;
    Palazzo Sacchetti 46;
    Palazzo Zuccari 33;
    San Giovanni in Laterano 30, 31;
    San Saba 16;
    Sant'Ignazio 51-53, 58, 59;
    Santi Domenico e Sisto 57;
    Sistine Chapel 44;
    Trinità dei Monti 83;
    Vatican Loggie 32;
    Villa Farnesina 38, 44.
ROSSI Gian Domenico (active 1755-1763) 62.
ROTTMAYR Johann Michael (1654-1730) 58-60.
RUBENS Peter Paul (1577-1640) 50.

Sabbioneta (Mantua), Assunta Church 56;
    Teatro Olimpico 60.
Salenegg Castle (Grisons) 73.
Saluzzo (Piedmont), Church of the Confraternità della Misericordia 62;
    Maresco Castle 69.
SALVIATI Francesco (1510-1563) 46.
SANSOVINO Jacopo (1486-1570) 48.
Sassuolo (Modena), Palazzo d'Este 75, 85.
SCAMOZZI Vincenzo (1552-1616) 69.
SCHÖNBORN, Counts of 52.
SCHWARZENBERG, Prince 87.
SEGA Giovanni del (died 1527) 19.
SERLIO Sebastiano (1475-1554) 38, 48-50, 67, 68.
SERRISTORI Umberto 90.

SERVANDONI Giovanni Niccolò (1695-1766) 70, 71.
SIGHIZZI Andrea (died 1684) 84.
SLUTER Claus (died 1405) 15.
Stupinigi (Piedmont) 61, 80, 81.
SUETONIUS (active c. A.D. 70-120) 12.

TACITUS (c. A.D. 55-after 116) 46.
TANZIO DA VARALLO (1576-c. 1655) 63.
TASSI Agostino (c. 1580-1644) 31, 40, 41, 52, 71, 72.
TEMPESTA Pietro (c. 1637-1701) 82.
TEUFEL Heinrich (died 1570) 49, 50.
TIBALDI Pellegrino (1527-1596) 42, 44, 45.
TIEPOLO Giambattista (1696-1770) 70.
TINTORETTO (1518-1594) 42.
TITIAN (c. 1490-1576) 38, 45, 48.

Trent, Council of (1545-1563) 44.
Trento (South Tyrol), Castle of Buonconsiglio 24, 25;
  Palazzo Geremia 48, 49.

Vaisseau Group, Geneva 97.
VALERIANI Domenico and Giuseppe (18th century) 61, 80, 81.
Varallo (Piedmont), Sacro Monte 63.
VARINI Felice (1952) 100.
VASARI Giorgio (1511-1574) 38, 44-46, 48.
Venice 48, 97;
  Palazzo Labia 70.
Verona (Venetia), Ferrari-Cartolari House 80, 87.
VERONESE Paolo (1528-1588) 38, 39, 103.
Versailles 72.

VICARIO Casimir 91.
Vienna, Court Chapel 68.
VIGNOLA Giacomo da (1507-1573) 43.
VINTLER Nikolaus 23.
VITRUVIUS POLLIO Marcus (active 46-30 BC) 10, 23, 38, 39, 70.
VITTONE Bernardo (1705-1770) 60-62.

Weingarten (Baden-Württemberg), Abbey Church 54, 55.
WENZLAUS, Master (active c. 1400) 24, 25.
WHITE Kenn 94, 95.
Wiesentheid (Franconia) 53.
WINCKELMANN Johann Joachim (1717-1768) 83.

ZUCCARI Federico (c. 1540-1609) 33.
ZWINGER Theodor 50.

SKIRA

Text and colour plates printed by
IRL Imprimeries Réunies Lausanne S.A.

Binding by
Reliure Veihl, Geneva

Printed in Switzerland